HOOCH

xxxxxxxxxxxxxxxxxxxxxxxx

Simplified Brewing,
Winemaking &
Infusing at Home

xxxxxxxxxxxxxxxxxxxxxxxx

SCOTT MEYER

RUNNING PRESS
PHILADELPHIA · LONDON

Books published by Running Press are available at special discounts for bulk purchases
in the United States by corporations, institutions, and other organizations. For more
information, please contact the Special Markets Department at the Perseus Books Group,
2300 Chestnut Street, Suite 200, Philadelphia, PA 19103, or call (800) 810-4145, ext. 5000,
or e-mail special.markets@perseusbooks.com.

ISBN 978-0-7624-4603-2
Library of Congress Control Number: 2012942523

E-book ISBN 978-0-7624-4829-6

9 8 7 6 5 4 3 2 1
Digit on the right indicates the number of this printing

Cover and interior design by Amanda Richmond
Edited by Kristen Green Wiewora
Typography: Archer, Franchise, and MailartRubberstamp

Running Press Book Publishers
2300 Chestnut Street
Philadelphia, PA 19103–4371

Visit us on the web!
www.runningpress.com

XXXXXXXXXXXXXXXXXXXXXXXXXX

TO MY VERY BEST FRIEND AND TRUE LOVE,
DAWN,
FOR ALL THOSE NIGHTS WE SMASHED FRUIT
AND IMAGINED OUR LIVES TOGETHER.

XXXXXXXXXXXXXXXXXXXXXXXXXX

CONTENTS

INTRODUCTION

HOOCH USED TO MEAN ROTGUT, SWILL, OLD GRAPE JUICE, FIREWATER, moonshine, and a lot of other unappealing terms for something you drink only because it's all there is or because you don't want to offend whoever is passing it your way. The new hooch is altogether different. It may be wine, beer, cider, mead, or spirits, and its purpose is not a quick and cheap buzz. It's made from ingredients raised with care and it's crafted with attention to quality from harvest to glass. Today's hooch is all about hands-on experience and the deep satisfaction of starting with a handful of seeds and turning them into a glassful of cheer you're proud to share.

Making your own hooch doesn't mean you are a bootlegger, cheapskate, or eccentric. Well, maybe you are a little of each. But when you grow (or gather) the ingredients, then handle them yourself every step of the way from raw material to bottle, you become an artisan with a great story you can offer along with the drink: This comes from right here; its *terroir* is my home. Not that you need a vineyard that stretches for acres or a vast cellar to grow and make a batch of brew, wine, or spirits. You can do something in a city apartment, a lot in a suburban backyard. You don't need to invest in expensive equipment to get started, and you can make drinks worth sharing even if you flunked chemistry in high school.

Transforming ordinary garden crops and foraged foods into sublime alcohol seems like it must be complicated, but it's remarkably easy. The earliest civilizations discovered—most likely by accident—how to make wine and beer. Medieval monks and farmers managed to produce drinks that inspired poetry and earned fortunes without really understanding how it happened. Today, we know that yeast has the unique ability to make alcohol from sugar, and researchers have documented the variations in each strain of yeast's reaction to different ingredients and conditions, making it simpler than ever before for anyone to capture nature's purest flavors in a bottle.

Ancient people surely appreciated—and often celebrated—the sacramental and intoxicating qualities of the alcohol they had. But they may have just as well valued fermenting and distilling—the processes of producing and concentrating alcoholic content—as a form of food preservation. (A really pleasurable kind of food preservation.) You can't overestimate the benefits of a safe supply of drinking liquids in times before sanitation made water a trustworthy option. We don't have to worry about a safe water supply anymore, but fermenting homegrown ingredients lets us capture and refine their flavors, and enjoy them for years after they are harvested.

Our world has been so shaped for our convenience, we can press a few buttons on our computers or phones, and anything we desire can be delivered right to our door. So why bother growing a garden? Why go to the trouble of making your own wines, brews, and spirits? I say it's worth it because the flavors of homegrown and homemade are the purest. Because you get to enjoy unique tastes that are not available commercially. Because many of us have discovered that something is missing from our convenient world. We are hungry for the genuine confidence that comes with providing for ourselves and we are thirsty for knowledge on how to do it simply. We're growing gardens because we love fresh food, we're preserving it to get a taste of homegrown food in every season, and we're sharing our bounty with family and friends because there is simple joy in offering your effort and care to those you love.

This book is meant to show you how easy and rewarding it is to grow and make your own hooch. I believe the goal is to enjoy the process as much as the outcome, so I've emphasized the most natural methods every step of the way and purity over convenience for each ingredient and additive. When sharing information on growing, I focus on the organic approach, not only because I know garden chemicals are toxic to people and the environment, but primarily because they leave behind residues that affect the flavor of your ingredients. (If you don't trust my admittedly biased opinion, ask any vintner or chef about that.) Likewise, I'm inclined to pass on adding sulfites when making my own hooch, though I realize many successful professionals and amateurs include them in their wines, ciders, and meads. I also prefer to use natural ingredients such as black tea and citrus fruits rather than purchase commercially produced tannins and acids. I don't intend to badger you with this point and I certainly won't condemn you if you find that you feel more confident relying on synthetic fertilizers and such purchased additives. I do hope you'll first try to do without them and trust that over time you will acquire the knowledge needed to keep your hooch pure from start to finish.

In the twenty-five years since I planted the first seeds in my own garden, I've gained so much insight on what will work in my conditions, both from talking to other gardeners and from my own experiences. Mostly, I've learned that I'll never stop learning, that every season is different than all the others, and that even if I dedicated all of my time and attention to my garden, there would always be new things to try and new insights to pick up.

The very same can be said for making hooch. The basics are very simple—as you'll see in this book—and you can expect to succeed on your first try. But as you become more familiar with the process, you can vary your ingredients and the choices you make along the way, learning how each affects the outcome and discovering the formulas that create the results you want. No matter how many batches you make, you will find there's always more to learn.

There is no substitute for trial-and-error learning, but, like gardeners, hooch crafters tend to be very generous with information and advice that can help you solve a problem. Local supply shops are not only a good place to purchase gear (while supporting a business in your community), they're also a fruitful place to meet and talk to people with more experience. The members of forums on such websites as www.homebrewtalk.com and www.winemakingtalking.com also eagerly answer questions and share their findings.

In researching this book and learning all I could about the best ways to ferment and distill homegrown ingredients, I was helped by many generous experts, and I am indebted to them all. A few deserving special note include Diane Flynt, Vince Shook, Paul Zimmerman, Harry Collins, Zeke Ferguson, Jeremy Kidde, Jason Grizzanti, and Christopher Boyd.

The research and writing of this book was encouraged and supported by Christopher Navratil at Running Press and nurtured and guided by Kristen Green Wiewora, an editor with boundless enthusiasm and invaluable insights. Right here, I raise a symbolic glass to toast both of them. I'm also grateful for the thoughtful design by Amanda Richmond, the diligent fact-checking of Louisa Hargrave, and the smart production work of Carolyn Sobczak and the rest of the team of the Perseus Books Group.

Last, and anything but least, I toast you, dear reader, for your time and attention. You could just buy a bottle or six-pack and switch on the Food Channel. But here you are (at the end of a book introduction, no less) and about to embark on an adventure in growing and making hooch just because you can. I can think of nothing more toast-worthy. Cheers!

CHAPTER № 1
FERMENTATION BASICS

FERMENTATION HAPPENS: IF YOU LEAVE A SOLUTION THAT CONTAINS sugar and water exposed to air, naturally occurring microbes will feast on the sugars and turn them into alcohol or (depending on the kind of sugar) into acids. Prehistoric people, and maybe many other creatures, must have discovered this transformation by accident and found that fermented foods and drinks were not only safe to eat, but beneficial in a variety of ways. They found that fermented honey, fruit, and grains were pleasurable to drink and had medicinal and even spiritual uses. The earliest civilizations had learned to manage the fermentation process and by the time of the classical Greek and Roman periods, making alcohol and fermented foods was commonplace. In fact, fermented beverages were essential for public health in places where people settled and polluted their own water supplies. Still, it was not until Louis Pasteur studied and explained the activity of yeast and bacteria in the 1860s that fermentation was clearly understood to be the result of yeast's digestion. Before Pasteur, fermentation was thought to be the result of spontaneous generation—a gift of God.

Fermenting is not just a way to make alcohol—it's a food preservation process. Fermenting milk into cheese and yogurt are ways to keep milk consumable longer, just as pickles and sauerkraut keep fresh cucumbers and cabbage edible well past the time when they would spoil. Fermentation unlocks the precursors to and reveals the flavors of fruit and grains, and preserves them for years after. Fermentation preserves food because the yeast reproduces faster than the undesirable microbes that cause spoilage, and then the alcohol or acids that are the result of fermentation reach levels that kill off all of the microbes, good and bad. Fermentation lets you safely—and deliciously—preserve a wide variety of homegrown ingredients, as you'll see throughout this book.

Fermenting is the first step to making stronger drinks, too. The raw ingredients in spirits such as brandy, apple jack, and bourbon are fermented to turn them into alcohol and then the alcohol and flavors are concentrated through distillation. We'll get into distilling in Chapter 6, but here we'll start with the basic information and steps to fermenting your garden-fresh foods.

⋈⋈⋈⋈⋈⋈⋈⋈ ESSENTIAL SUPPLIES ⋈⋈⋈⋈⋈⋈⋈⋈

Home fermenting can become a costly hobby, but it doesn't have to be expensive when you are starting out. You do, however, need a few basic items to get started. Search online and at local supply stores; you may find well-cared-for used equipment that will serve your needs as you learn more about what works for you.

BASIC GEAR

Moist, sugar-rich ingredients left in any container will begin to ferment, but when you want a predictably palatable result, it helps to have some simple, low-cost gear to help you stay on track. Most crucial, unless you protect the fermented beverages from oxygen, spoilage bacteria will turn your homegrown ingredients into vinegar, not alcohol. The items here are useful whether you're making wine, cider, or mead. They also work for making beer, but that requires few more essential items that are covered in the chapter on brewing (page 26).

PRIMARY FERMENTER. When blending all of your ingredients and pitching the yeast, you'll find it easiest to work in a container with a wide open top, like a food-grade plastic bucket. Beware of non-food-grade garbage cans, which may be treated with rat poison. A 6-gallon container is ideal, because it gives you plenty of room to make manageable batches from 1 to 5 gallons. Considering that a gallon of liquid weighs about 8 pounds, anything larger is too heavy to manage. You can buy plastic buckets designed for home fermenters, which have gallon markings indicating the volume levels and an opening drilled and plugged where a spigot can be inserted. If you get any other container—and you can find lots of suitable, food-grade buckets that are discarded by restaurants and other food-service operations—you can mark the levels yourself and drill out a hole for the spigot. Just be wary of any bucket that has many nicks and scratches where bacteria can colonize.

Primary Fermenter

As you will read in greater detail in the section on oxygen (page 26), you can choose to allow your must to be exposed to the air during the active primary fermentation, though it does risk contamination by acetic acid bacteria (the kind that make vinegar) and other undesirable microbes that derail the yeast's work. As long as the surface shows a head of bubbles, there is typically enough CO_2 evolving from the fermentation to blanket the must or wort (the liquid that becomes wine, cider, mead, or beer) and protect it from the oxygen needed by acetic acid bacteria to survive. You want to at least cover it with a cheesecloth to keep bugs and debris out. For a safer, closed fermentation, get a bucket with a tight lid that can be fitted with a fermentation lock.

SECONDARY FERMENTER. Glass carboys—large jugs with a narrow opening—are the choice for secondary fermentation of nearly every experienced home brewer and vintner. The carboy's design is ideal for fermentation because it minimizes the amount of oxygen that comes in contact with the must. The cone-shaped top traps nitrogen, which forms a natural barrier to oxygen.

Carboys are commonly available in 1-, 3-, 5- and 6-gallon sizes. You can find them at yard sales and flea markets, as well as from online and retail suppliers like those listed in Resources on page 195. If you buy them used, be sure they have no cracks or chips. Get clean new caps for them.

When full, glass carboys can weigh 50 pounds or more. They're hard to handle and are destroyed (along with your product) if they break. Rubber handles designed for them, available from brewing/winemaking suppliers make them easier to manage. Sitting them in large plastic milk crates works well, too. This protects them from separating at the base, as they may do if stored on a hard surface, such as concrete. If they separate when you pick them up at the base, you may lose a finger.

Secondary Fermenter

AIRLOCK. While you want to keep your must or wort from exposure to air during fermentation, you also need to let the carbon dioxide that is produced escape. An airlock, also referred to as a fermentation lock or a bubbler, makes that easiest. It's a plastic or glass tube with a few twists and turns in it, with a rubber stopper (called a bung) with a hole that the tube fits into it. You keep the tube filled with distilled water or clear alcohol like vodka to prevent any microbes—or fruit flies—from getting down the tube and into your must or wort. Vodka keeps the airlock more sterile than water does, but it evaporates faster so you have to replenish it more often. If you go with water, refresh it every few days to prevent any microbes from getting established. No matter which you use, be sure there is always enough liquid in the airlock to be effective. An airlock also is a good indicator of continuing fermentation because the liquid in it will bubble (hence the term *bubbler*).

An airlock isn't very expensive—you can get a basic plastic one for about $15 or delicate blown-glass models with more handy features for about $100—but if you're on a tight budget when just starting out you can fashion a crude one by placing one end of a sanitized tube into the rubber stopper and keeping the other end fully submerged in a small cup of water.

FLEXIBLE PLASTIC TUBING. Transferring your fermented drink from one container to another is called racking and in that process you separate the liquid from its sediment—dead yeast and debris from your raw ingredients—so that the liquid becomes clearer. You make the transfer with flexible plastic tubing. A 6-foot length is usually sufficient, but you might want to get several lengths if you plan to ferment often because the tubing needs to be replaced as it ages. You can buy it from a brewing supplier or pick it up at a hardware store or home center. Just be sure it is labeled "food grade." The standard tubing sizes are $3/8$ inch and $1/2$ inch. Clamps for both ends of the tube will help you control the flow of liquid and minimize messy accidents. It takes a little practice to get used to handling the tubing, so keep in mind that the end should never touch the floor.

HYDROMETER. A valuable tool for accurately reading how your fermentation process is progressing, a hydrometer measures the relative density of liquids to water, which is sometimes referred to as specific gravity (SG). (I'll explain this in more detail on page 23.)

The standard hydrometer design for brewers and vintners is made of glass and has a long, cylindrical stem with a small bulb at the bottom containing a little lead ball. Markings on the side show the SG measurement. Basic models cost about $15, those with more features go for $40 or more.

The hydrometer works on the principle that a floating body displaces a volume of liquid whose weight is equal to its own; the lighter the liquid (that is, the less its SG), the deeper the body sinks because a greater amount of liquid is required to equal the body's weight. When you use your hydrometer, keep in mind that temperature affects the readings, because water becomes denser as it cools. Be sure you do all of your testing at room temperature or use a thermometer with an adjustment chart. If you become more serious about fermenting, you may want to have two or three hydrometers with different ranges for more precision. Those that measure the 5 percent to –2 percent range are especially useful at the end of fermentation.

BOTTLES, CORKER, OR CAPPER. You can buy bottles from beer or wine supply stores, but you can also clean thoroughly and reuse empties from family and friends, or ask for them at local bars and restaurants. For wine, pass on screw-top bottles because they can't be corked. Champagne bottles are made of thicker glass, so they hold up well under pressure. However, you need specific corks and wire for them. Beer bottles come in so many shapes these days, but the tops tend to be the same size.

Light is no friend of your homemade beer, wine, mead, or cider. You might like to see how it looks as it ages, but light can spoil its flavor and change its color. Avoid clear glass and stick with green or brown bottles. Wine left exposed to sunlight in a clear glass bottle will smell like rotten garlic.

You don't have to bother taking the labels off used bottles, but if you want to, get a hair dryer and hold it near the label to soften the glue behind it. After you peel it away, scrape off any glue or paper left behind with an X-Acto knife or razor blade. Pure acetone nail polish remover is useful to dissolve the residual glue.

You can find a little plastic device to help you insert corks into bottles for $10 or you could opt for the $2,300 pneumatic corker, but if you're making and bottling 5-gallon batches, a $30 floor corker is about right. Wear safety glasses when corking, as some bottles are imperfect and break under the pressure of corking.

Cappers for beer bottles have about the same price range and again for about $30 you can get a sturdy and easy-to-use model. If you are tempted to store wine in beer bottles, be aware that wine is acidic and will corrode the cap, and subsequently will taste rusty.

ADDITIVES. Grapes, cider apples, and malted grains have a balance of flavors that yield great-tasting drinks after fermentation. But many other raw ingredients—including most fruits and vegetables, as well as honey—lack sufficient acidity or the bite of tannins that those more common ingredients have naturally. You need to add those components to your must, or you may end up with a result only you are willing to drink. Keep in mind that microbes that harm humans can't survive at a pH under 4.0. You can buy premixed acid blends (follow the package directions for amounts) or you can simply use freshly squeezed lemon juice. Use the juice from one-half to a whole medium-size lemon in each gallon of must, depending on how acidic the raw ingredients are. Strawberries and most vegetables are closer to neutral, so they need more lemon juice, while raspberries and tomatoes need less. Remember to always mix acids into your must before you pitch the yeast.

Tannins are an essential flavor component of all but the sweetest wines, and they're not naturally present in almost any fresh food except grapes and apples. So you need to add them, but because the flavor is noticeably bitter, you want to add only small amounts. You can buy powdered tannin blend, often made from dried grape pomace, or you can add black tea to your must. The blacker and stronger the tea, the better. If you add tannin powder to red wine before it ferments, it will combine with protein in the must and stabilize the naturally occurring tannins, making the color more even and the flavors softer.

Pectins are compounds in many fruits that help them to gel, which is desirable when you're making jam but not when you're fermenting. You'll see in the section on making wine that pectic enzyme is recommended with some fruits—the enzyme breaks up the pectins before they can set and ruin your drink. Pectic enzyme also breaks down cell walls, releasing more of the fruits' flavor compounds. You can buy it in liquid or powdered form—the latter costs less, does not need to be refrigerated and is sufficiently effective for making small batches of wine. If you add sulfites to your wine (more on that in the next paragraph), wait at least ten hours after before mixing in the pectic enzyme.

CAMPDEN TABLETS. Commercial winemakers and many home fermenters rely on campden tablets (potassium metabisulfite) to kill off wild yeasts and other unwelcome microbes that accompany fruit from the field to the fermentation bucket. The sulfite is also used to stop fermentation before the yeast has consumed all of the sugar, giving the tightest control over the sweetness and alcohol content. It is also added during the secondary fermentation period to protect the drink from oxidation. It's sold in tablet form, with each containing about one-half gram of the compound. Sulfites reduce your risk of spoilage but some people have allergic reactions to them, others say they can taste the residues in the finished product. For me, the natural way is almost always the best—take care of the ingredients from harvest to fermentation bucket, be diligent about sanitation and airspace while you are fermenting and you can make wine without sulfites. Many winemakers who know the source of their fruit opt not to use sulfites before fermentation, but do use them at bottling if the wine will be aged over six months. Sulfite is the only substance known to protect wine from both oxidation and from bacterial spoilage.

Be aware that sulfites, sulfates, and sulfides are entirely different chemicals. If you can eat a "golden" raisin or a fig Newton without an allergic reaction, you're not allergic to sulfites.

HANDY ACCESSORIES

The gear covered in the preceding section is essential (except for the sulfites). It's possible to do without some of the items, but not easily. The stuff in this section may not be necessary, but each item can help you to be more successful. You can add them to your kit as your interest and time investment grow. They are listed in the order of how helpful they are.

PH METER. Acidity level is so crucial to the effective functioning of yeast. You'll get a lot of reassurance that your must or wort is on track if you check the pH before you start fermenting. Knowing the pH will tell you not how much acid you have, but how much is in an active, ionized state. Such minerals as potassium can "buffer" the acids, raising the pH to the point where bacterial spoilage is possible, leaving the drink flat tasting and off-color. Old-fashioned pH test strips work, but a multi-feature electronic meter with thermometer included gives you lots of valuable information you can use throughout the process. A good one can cost $75 or more, but you'll use it often. If you do use a meter, standardize it often for accurate readings.

pH Meter

RACKING CANE. The aim of racking your drink, or moving it from one container to another, is to separate the liquid from the dead yeast and other sediment in the container. A racking cane attaches to flexible tubing and is curved on the end that goes into the full container—it keeps the tube from resting on the bottom, where the sediment is concentrated. The handiest racking canes have a siphon included so you can generate suction to start liquid flowing.

Racking Cane

FRESH FRUIT PROCESSORS. Large-scale operations have equipment for turning fresh fruit into juice, but you don't need to set up a manufacturing plant to make processing fruit easier and cleaner for you. You can find fruit presses that fit in a basement or garage for less than $500 and a crusher/destemmer that can sit on a tabletop for around $200. Both allow you to speed up the process significantly. Juicers and pitters also help and may be found at yard sales and flea markets. Pulp bags and strainers make it easier to extract the flavor from a wide variety of fruit, vegetables, and herbs while keeping particles that can mar the flavor or clarity out of your must.

REFRACTOMETER. A handheld device that measures how light refracts through a liquid, a refractometer is often used by wine and cider makers to assess the sugar content of fruit. This is a standardized way of determining ripeness. To use it, a sample of juice is placed between a calibrated prism and a covering plate, then the refractometer is held up to your eye, allowing you to see a line on the scale marked inside. There are many different models—you want to be sure to get one with automatic temperature compensation, because changes in temperature affect the readings.

BOTTLE FILLERS. Funnels and tubes let you fill one bottle at a time, which won't take too long with a batch of 5 gallons. But if you start to make bigger batches or want to keep the bottling process cleaner and easier, get a three- or five-spout bottle filler. It's compact enough to fit into a garage or basement.

BOTTLE BRUSHES AND BOTTLE TREES. In the next section, I will cover the absolutely critical topic of sanitation, but while we're on the subject of handy accessories, a selection of different-size brushes and a rubber tree for drying bottles upside down help you ensure that the bottles you plan to use are as clean as can be.

✕✕✕✕✕✕✕✕ SERIOUS ABOUT SANITIZING ✕✕✕✕✕✕✕✕

I asked the same question of every one of the many experienced fermenters I talked to in researching this book: What is the most important lesson you've learned since you started out? Surprisingly—or maybe not so surprisingly—they all gave the same basic answer as their first response: Lapses in sanitation are far more likely to spoil your efforts than any other cause. When bacteria come in contact with your must or wort, they can compete with yeast and totally derail the fermentation process. Even just a few stray microbes in a bottle can produce off-flavors.

To prevent that, you must sanitize and thoroughly dry every single surface and implement that will come in contact with the fluid. That includes not just the fermentation buckets, carboys, and bottles, but also the siphon, funnel, tubing, bung, airlock, measuring cups, spoons, and your hands. And you need to repeat the careful cleaning every time you use your gear. Wiping things with a sponge or cloth is more likely to introduce new bacteria than to remove them. Air dry, always!

SOAP AND WATER. You can use very hot water and liquid soap to clean your fermenting equipment. You want to take extra care to rinse thoroughly, because soap clings to many surfaces and can leave behind a residue that could be a fertile breeding ground for bacteria. Use the purest unscented dish soap (e.g., Ivory) to keep any odors from lingering behind and finding their way into the drink. Unscented baking soda is a good soap alternative, too.

You might think that using your kitchen's automatic dishwasher is an effective way to sanitize. It uses very hot water and soap to clean and warm air dries the dishes inside. But be wary of this approach—a dishwasher gets your plates and glasses clean enough to eat from, but it can leave some bacteria alive and soap residue may not be thoroughly rinsed off. Unless you have a commercial-grade dishwasher with a power booster, your water won't get hot enough to truly sanitize.

BLEACH. Even better than soap at killing bacteria, unscented chlorine laundry bleach diluted in water (five parts water to one part bleach) is the most popular way to sanitize gear used for fermenting. It is widely available and very effective. Some pros find that it can leave behind an aftertaste, especially if you are not thorough enough with rinsing. I also have to note here that chlorine is a toxic chemical that harms the environment both in its production and when you dispose of it.

Oxygen bleach, also known as hydrogen peroxide, is a very effective antimicrobial sanitizer. It's a bit more expensive than chlorine bleach, but less prone to unpleasant aftertastes. Remember, though, it's not for cleaning out residue from used bottles, buckets, and carboys—it works just as a sanitizer *after* cleaning.

ALCOHOL. For the spot sanitizing of small items like tools and valves, ordinary household rubbing (isopropyl) alcohol is effective. Keep a spray bottle with a solution of three parts alcohol to one part water handy when you're involved in the fermentation process, so you can use it as needed.

SANITIZERS. Professional brewers and vintners, along with a lot of bars and other businesses that need sanitary glassware, rely on products formulated to clean thoroughly and leave behind no residues or odors. There are a variety of these acid-based cleaners on the market, but the most popular and widely available are B-Brite, C-Brite, and Star San. They are similar, though not identical, but the latter was the most recommended by experts I've spoken to. These products neutralize lees (dead or residual yeast that drops to the bottom of the fermenter) and mineral deposits left behind by water and other ingredients, and they kill bacteria and other microbes. In most cases, sanitizing products need no final rinse to remove residues—you just pour them off after they're done foaming. This keeps new bacteria from colonizing in water droplets left behind by rinsing. Sanitizers are more costly than household products, but if you can afford them, you get it back in protection against wasting what you invest in ingredients if they are spoiled by less than pristine gear.

Sanitizing is important at all times. I could mention it with every step or direction in this book and it still wouldn't be as often as you need to do it. But I'm only going to say it once—right here. Every time you get ready to start a batch, sanitize all of your gear right before you begin. When the batch is finished, thoroughly clean and dry the gear, then sanitize before you pack it away. Before you start the next batch, whenever that is, sanitize it again. And again. You get the idea—don't waste your time fermenting if you don't have the time to sanitize.

✕✕✕✕✕✕✕✕✕✕✕✕✕✕ WATER ✕✕✕✕✕✕✕✕✕✕✕✕✕✕

Your most basic supply is water. It makes up more than 90 percent of any drink you make, so it has a significant impact on the flavor of your finished product. (That's why one of the major American beer companies likes to promote its "Rocky Mountain" water, even for the product it brews in Virginia, Ohio, and Texas.) For most of us, water from the tap is not an ideal choice. Tap water is often too acidic for healthy fermentation because many municipalities treat it with chlorine and other chemicals to kill unwelcome microbes. Soft water—created by processing hard water through salts and other compounds—may end up with a distinct metallic taste and can be too alkaline for fermentation. Distilled water is pure and has a neutral pH, but it lacks mineral content that yeast needs. It is, in a sense, too dead for yeast to survive in it.

The ideal is true spring water, because it has minerals, but no additives that affect pH or the flavor of your finished drink. These days, few of us have direct access to a spring from which we can collect water. You most likely will be buying spring water in bottles. Look for "ozonated" spring water, which has been purified of bacteria and other contaminants using oxygen molecules stimulated by ultraviolet light rather than with harsh chemicals. Deer Park and Volvic are two trustworthy brands of spring water.

If I promise not to give you disturbing flashbacks to high-school chemistry class, will you stay with me here as I explain how fermentation works? When you get to managing the process on your own, you'll be glad you did.

Start with this: Fermenting fresh food and water is the digestive process of yeast, which consumes carbohydrates (e.g., sugar), excretes alcohol and acids, and emits carbon dioxide. The yeast converts the sugars in the food into glucose ($C_6H_{12}O_6$), and then breaks down the glucose molecules in a ten-step sequence called glycolysis. The result of the process is two molecules of ethyl alcohol (CH_3CH_2OH) and two molecules of carbon dioxide (CO_2). Your chemistry teacher might have written it as this formula: $C_6H_{12}O_6 = 2(CH_3CH_2OH) + 2(CO_2)$.

When you add yeast to a sugar-rich fluid you've made, you initiate a life cycle in which the yeast reproduce madly, get their fill of sugar and then die. I won't give you all the lurid details of their short and busy existence, but it will help you to guide yeast to do your bidding if you are familiar with these four distinct stages of their lives:

FUEL UP. When you first pitch the yeast into a must (for wine, cider, and mead) or wort (for beer), it takes on oxygen, gathers nutrients, and undergoes cellular changes that prepare it to reproduce. This "lag time" can last from twelve to seventy-two hours, depending on the specific strain of yeast. In the most commonly used yeasts, the lag time will be over in about twenty-four hours.

REPRODUCTION. You'll know when lag time has ended when the must or wort is bubbling vigorously, which typically continues for four to six days for most types of drinks. During this next, "aerobic" phase, the yeast is reproducing multiple times until it reaches a peak defined by the amount of sugar, nutrients, and oxygen available in the must or wort. There typically are more than a quadrillion yeast organisms per quart when they begin to metabolize the sugar.

CONSUMPTION. When reproduction has peaked, the slower, steadier part of the process starts. In the case of cider, this fermentation stage may reach its natural conclusion in four to six weeks, whereas mead may be fermented in about eight weeks. For wine and beer, this primary fermentation can take three to four months, and in certain formulas even longer.

DECLINE. The final stage, known as flocculation, arrives when the sugar supply has dwindled and the alcohol content of the fluid is too high for most of the yeast to survive. As they run out of steam, the yeast cells clump together in "flocs" and fall to the bottom of the container. As this occurs, the fluid begins to clear. But even while most of the yeast is in decline, some of them remain active in the must or wort, continuing the conversion of sugars to alcohol for another three to six months or even longer.

SPECIFIC GRAVITY

Although you can't actually see all of this process without a microscope, you can observe visible signs that it's happening, such as bubbling and the floc clumps on the bottom of your containers. Those signs give you a general idea of where you are in the process. You also want to take precise measurements along the way to guide you and assure you that the process is working as it should. The most crucial of those measurements is the fluid's sugar content at various stages of the cycle. You can use one of several systems to calculate this, including Brix (the choice of professional vintners), Balling degrees, and Plato (used mostly by brewers). The most dependable way to check the specific gravity is with a hydrometer. Pure water at 68°F has a gravity of 1.000. Your must or wort, a fluid comparatively dense with solids, will have a higher gravity, in some cases up to 1.140. As the sugar is metabolized by the yeast, the fluid's density, or gravity, decreases.

Now let's go back to our formula. The yeast turns glucose into two ethyl alcohol molecules and two carbon dioxide molecules. During fermentation, the CO_2 escapes as it bubbles away, while the alcohol is left behind. By comparing the molecular weight of carbon dioxide (44.0098) with that of ethyl alcohol (46.0688), you find that for each gram of CO_2 that bubbles off, you have 1.05 grams of alcohol. You can measure the amount of alcohol your fluid has by taking a gravity reading at the start of fermentation and at different junctures along the way.

For instance, imagine that the starting gravity of your fluid is 1.06 and after fermentation the gravity is 1.02. Subtract the ending gravity from the starting and you'll know how much carbon dioxide gassed off. Multiply the difference (0.04 kilograms/liter) by 1.05 and you get the mass of the alcohol, in this case 0.042 kg/L. Now that you know both the mass of the solution (1.02 kg/L) and the mass of the alcohol (0.042 kg/L) you can calculate the percentage of alcohol by mass by dividing the two. I'll do the math here: 0.042 divided by 1.02 equals 0.041, which means the fluid is 4.1 percent alcohol by mass. When you measure the alcohol in beer, wine, and other drinks, you want to know the alcohol by volume rather than mass—that's what "ABV" means when you see it on labels of liquor you buy. The percentage of alcohol by mass is higher than the percentage of alcohol by volume because an equal mass of alcohol occupies more volume than water does. You can convert the percent of alcohol by mass to percent of alcohol by volume by dividing the mass into the density of alcohol, which is 0.79 g/L at room temperature. To follow through on our example, you divide 4.1 alcohol by mass by 0.79, which gets you 5.2 percent alcohol by volume, or about the alcohol content of cider or medium-strength beer.

All of this information is important for choosing the right yeast for your recipe and the end result you desire. Fortunately, there are tools to help you do this. A hydrometer is a simple device that measures the gravity in a fluid. You take your first reading before you pitch the yeast and then at regular intervals along the way. You'll know the fermentation process is nearly or completely finished when the gravity stays the same for several consecutive weeks. (Find out more about hydrometers on page 14.)

The denser your must—that is, the more sugars and other ingredients it has—the higher the starting gravity will be. Each strain of yeast has an optimal gravity level and limits to its alcohol tolerance. If you use yeast that is outside of its tolerance, the fermentation process will stall before finishing, leaving you with an unpalatable drink and wasted ingredients. Every yeast strain's optimal gravity and tolerance are available from yeast suppliers. You will find out more on pages 30 to 33 about how to choose your yeast to match your recipe and the alcohol level you want.

It's a good rule of thumb that you can expect the gravity of a must or wort to drop by at most about 0.100 points during the fermentation process. With that in mind, you can narrow down the yeast options for it and anticipate roughly what the alcohol content will be when it's finished.

pH

The right gravity may be the most important factor in getting yeast to function effectively, but it's not the only one. The must also needs the right pH, a supply of oxygen at the start and a consistent source of nutrients.

Technically a measure of potential hydrogen, pH is a way to gauge the comparative acidity or alkalinity of a compound, on a scale of 0 to 14, with 0 being purely acidic and 14 being all alkaline. Pure water has a neutral pH of 7, and pure alcohol is close to that. Water that's been treated with chlorine to purify it (as many municipalities do) has an acidic pH. Many of the ingredients used in fermenting to make alcohol, such as fruit juice, grain mash, and honey, are also distinctly acidic. They can bring the must's pH down below 6.0 and even lower. Furthermore, you may add acids (e.g., citric, malic, or tartaric) to your recipes, separately or in a blend, to help balance the powerful sweetness of such ingredients as honey or those that lack sufficient natural acids, such as dandelions. Many strains of yeast do not stay active when the pH is 5.0 or lower.

Determining the pH of your must or wort is a lot easier than explaining what it is or how it works. You can use a litmus test (which in this case is literal and not the metaphor so overused today in politics and culture). A real litmus test involves dipping treated strips of paper into the fluid. If the strips turn red, the fluid is acidic; if the strip turns blue, then the fluid is alkaline. It is, however, a rather broad measure of the acidity. You get a more specific reading using metallic precision strips or an electronic pH meter, both of which are also more expensive than the simple strips. The more precise reading helps you to know exactly how close you are to the intolerance range for your yeast and can guide you in bringing the fluid into the acceptable range.

You can find yeast that can handle the acidic environment or you can raise the pH by adding to the liquid base (another way of saying *alkaline*) substances, such as calcium carbonate (also known as chalk). You want to use these cautiously, though, because they can drastically alter the acid-to-base ratio and push your pH too far in the wrong direction. They also can leave behind undesirable flavors. Add these compounds a teaspoon at a time to a small portion of your must or wort, mixing it well with the rest of the must or wort, then take a pH reading before you add more.

OXYGEN

In the lag time right after you pitch yeast, the cells begin preparing themselves for the rapid and expansive reproduction they undertake before they begin metabolizing the sugars you've provided for them. To make the changes they need to reproduce—which they do by dividing into new yeast cells—they need a healthy supply of oxygen. Scientists who study this process estimate that they need about eight to twelve parts per million in the must or wort. Although measuring oxygen concentration in fluid requires laboratory equipment, a home fermenter can simply inject a sufficient amount of oxygen into the fluid by stirring it vigorously before pitching the yeast. More advanced brewers and those who want more control can use an air stone or bubbler, such as those used in aquariums, to inject oxygen into the fluid. About ten minutes of aerating with a bubbler will saturate the fluid with enough oxygen for the yeast cells to reproduce.

Once the primary fermentation begins, yeast reproduction gradually tapers off. During those first few days of vigorous fermenting, the yeast still needs oxygen, but much less. For that reason, some pros now advocate leaving the fluid exposed to the air, from which it can draw oxygen, for three or four days after primary fermentation begins. You need to protect it, however, from airborne impurities and wild yeasts that will compete with the yeast you've selected. If your fluid is in a bucket, you can cover it tightly (leaving no open areas) with cheesecloth or other air-permeable fabric. If you're starting in a carboy or other container with a limited opening, you can simply stuff cotton into it to block out everything else but air.

After this initial period when the yeast has a high demand for the oxygen it needs to reproduce, oxygen then becomes an enemy of successful fermentation. Once the fluid is bubbling away, you want to prevent it from oxidizing, which can create stale flavors in your drink. Rather, you are encouraging anaerobic fermentation, which means it has no exposure to air. An airlock on your fermenting vessels is a simple mechanism that allows the carbon dioxide (the *oxide* is *oxygen*) created by the metabolizing of sugar to escape while allowing no more air in.

FEEDING

Yeast feeds on the sugar in your must or wort, but the carbohydrates in sugar do not provide all of the nutrients that it needs for healthy, consistent fermentation. Nitrogen, the vital element you need to grow plants in your garden, is essential for yeasts to do their work, too. Nitrogen helps the yeasts produce the natural enzymes they require for metabolizing sugar. A sufficient amount of nitrogen bolsters the yeasts' tolerance to alcohol, so they will keep converting sugar even as the alcohol level in the drink rises. Minerals, such as zinc, calcium, and magnesium are important, too. Lipids, the scientific name for fats, are also needed by yeast cells to reproduce efficiently.

The traditional alcohol-making ingredients, malted grains and such fruit as grapes and apples, typically contain a sufficient supply of nutrients for fermentation, though the levels can vary depending on the raw ingredients. Honey has much lower quantities of these critical nutrients—generally, the darker the honey, the more minerals it has, but even then the amounts are still too close to, if not below, the necessary levels. Without enough of all the key nutrients, the yeast won't be able to reproduce in sufficient multiples and will stop metabolizing the sugar. When you're just learning to make your own alcohol—with any raw ingredients—you increase your chances of success by including yeast nutrients in the must or wort. Free amino nitrogen (FAN) is the form of nitrogen that yeasts use most efficiently. Scientists who have studied yeast life cycle and fermentation have found that 300 to 500 milligrams of nitrogen per liter of must or wort is the optimal concentration. Diammonium phosphate is a widely available form of FAN, sold by brewing and winemaking suppliers. It's often labeled simply "yeast nutrient" or "DAP."

A better choice, especially for beginners, is a set of nutrients blended specifically for the type of fermentation you're doing. Fermaid K from Lalvin and Superfood from Red Star are two widely available products. Along with nitrogen, they also contain micronutrients, such as magnesium and zinc, which may, depending on your ingredients, be in short supply in the must or wort.

The terms *yeast nutrient* and *yeast energizer* are often used interchangeably, but they are slightly different. The latter may contain a variety of nutrients, but it also typically includes yeast hulls, also known as yeast ghosts. They are cell walls cast off during the reproductive cycle. Two fatty acids formed during fermentation, decanoic and octanoic acids, are toxic to yeast. When the concentration of those acids reaches a critical level, the yeast levels drop and the fermentation process slows. Yeast hulls absorb much of the fatty acids, keeping them from reaching the toxic level. Adding yeast energizer with the hulls included to your must or wort is insurance against the acids reaching the critical level. Researchers have found that about 0.2 to 0.3 grams of yeast hulls per liter of fluid are enough to manage the acids effectively. As with the nutrients, yeast energizer is especially critical whenever you make mead and wines with fruits and vegetables (other than grapes).

One of the most noticeable signs that the yeast did not have a sufficient supply of nutrients and hulls is the smell of rotten eggs that indicates the presence of hydrogen sulfide (H_2S). This can be caused by other factors as well—including an overuse of sulfur dust to protect fruit from rot while it's still growing—but if you have noticed the sulfur odor during fermentation, you can try to eliminate it by racking the must or wort and let it splash as you do to help dissipate the unwanted sulfides. For your next batch with the same ingredients, be sure to include yeast energizer.

✕✕✕✕✕✕✕✕✕✕ YEAST HUSBANDRY ✕✕✕✕✕✕✕✕✕✕

Earlier in this chapter I explained how fermentation works and the critical conditions needed to stimulate fermentation. Now let's get to know the most important actors in the process a little better. Yeasts are one-celled microbes related to fungi, and there are 1,500 known species. The vast majority of yeasts are wild, but a few species have been cultivated by people for making bread as well as brewing since at least the time of the ancient Egyptians.

One species, *Saccharomyces cerevisiae*, is the most widely used for making wine, mead, cider, and many types of beer, and for baking. Hundreds of different strains of the species are available to home vintners and brewers, and each has a unique set of attributes, such as its temperature and alcohol tolerances. Whenever you ferment, you want to choose a strain of yeast with attributes that will produce the results

you're aiming for with the ingredients you're giving it. If that sounds complicated, don't worry; there's more on that coming up.

A few other yeast species are used to produce alcohol. *S. pastorianus* (formerly known as *S. carlsbergesis*) is used to make lager beers and *S. bayanus* is a popular option for cider and white wines. Brewers of lambic and other Belgian-style beers work with a small group of other yeasts in the genus *Brettanomyces*. The *Brettanomyces* yeasts, however, are an enemy of good wine; they produce barnyard aromas and flavors after they ferment grapes.

Many winemakers, including those who create the most exceptional wines, do work with the indigenous yeasts that form on grape skins. Those yeast strains have coevolved with the grapes during the thousands of years since people began cultivating both the fruit and microbe. But working with wild yeasts is not for the beginner or the risk averse.

As yeast converts sugar to alcohol and carbon dioxide, it also produces flavor and aroma compounds with technical sounding names, such as esters, phenols, and ketones. Esters bring the fruity flavors; phenols, the spicier notes. Each combination of yeast strain and raw ingredients produces its own unique balance of these compounds. Getting that combination right and managing it attentively makes all the difference between what's merely drinkable and the truly sublime. For instance, the most common ketone, diacetyl, can make brew taste buttery, but it oxidizes quickly and leaves behind a stale-tasting drink.

In optimal conditions, yeast produces ethyl alcohol, with its sharp, sweet bite of flavor. When the temperature is too high during fermentation, the pH of the must or wort is low, or nutrients are in short supply, yeast produces fusel alcohol, a heavier compound with a sharper bite that tastes of solvent. It's reputed to contribute to hangovers, though there doesn't seem to be research to support that. A bit of fusel alcohol is a welcome part of the flavor of some ales and ciders, but is most unwelcome in wine and mead.

CHOOSING A STRAIN

Most home vintners and brewers stick with the countless strains of *S. cerevisiae* available to them. These strains have been cultivated and categorized for either beer or wine, and some specifically for cider and mead are now on the market, too. There is more on those strains of *S. cerevisiae* in the chapters on making cider and mead. Four companies offer a wide selection of different strains to choose from: Red Star, Lalvin, Wyeast, and White Labs. There are others, but these brands offer yeasts for everything from champagne to cider, porter to mead, in package sizes for fermenting in 5-gallon batches.

Your choice of yeast strain begins with what kind of drink you want to produce—from very sweet to extra dry, to fruity to acidic, to low to high in alcohol. Each strain of yeast has its own unique combination of attributes. You match the yeast to your ingredients to create the final result. The key qualities you need to know about yeast are its attenuation, flocculation, ideal temperature, and alcohol tolerance.

ATTENUATION. Yeast strains vary in the percentage of sugar they consume during fermentation—the percentage is known as its attenuation. Most common yeast strains attenuate at 65 to 80 percent of the sugar. The higher the attenuation, the drier, or less sweet, the drink becomes. For dry wine, cider, and mead, you want almost 100 percent attenuation, but less than 75 percent for sweet wines.

Understanding each yeast's attenuation range helps you create exactly the kind of drink you want and lets you determine exactly when fermentation has peaked. To figure out whether a yeast has finished, you need to know the original gravity (OG) of your must or wort, which you measure with a hydrometer before you pitch the yeast. When the bubbling of fermentation has slowed or almost stopped, take a sample of your drink and measure it again with the hydrometer to determine the final gravity (FG). With those numbers and this formula, you can calculate the attenuation percentage:

$$[(OG - FG)/(OG - 1)] \times 100 = \% \textbf{ ATTENUATION}$$

You can go to page 14 to get up to speed on specific gravity and hydrometers.

You'll see an expected attenuation range listed with each yeast strain. When the yeast you've used reaches its expected attenuation percentage, you'll know it has finished fermenting.

ALCOHOL TOLERANCE. Like all of us, yeast strains vary in their alcohol tolerance. There are lightweights and those that can just hang in long after others have given up. Really, I'm referring to yeast. As the yeast processes the sugars in the must or wort, the percentage of alcohol in the solution increases. The yeast continues the conversion of sugar into alcohol until the concentration is too high for the yeast to survive. The percentage of alcohol in the solution at which the yeast dies is its alcohol tolerance.

A yeast strain's alcohol tolerance is critical because it directly affects both the sweetness and potency of your final result. How much, if any, sugar is left in your drink depends on how much the yeast was able to consume before the alcohol level killed it off. And if you want to produce very strong drinks, including spirits, you need yeast that can continue fermenting even when the alcohol level is very high.

When you buy yeast, you'll see the alcohol tolerance of each strain. It may be as low as 2 percent or as high (in rare cases) as more than 20 percent, with most falling between 8 and 16 percent. Remember, though, that the alcohol tolerance is not the alcohol by volume (ABV) that we commonly use to refer to a drink's potency. (Check back in the "Gravity" section of this chapter, page 24, for an explanation.)

OPTIMAL TEMPERATURE AND PH. Yeast strains perform differently as the temperatures change. Fermentation goes slowly in cool conditions and may cease before you have the flavor and alcohol level you want. In too-warm conditions, yeast tends to produce off-flavored compounds and burn itself out early. Your must or wort needs to be within the yeast's temperature range when you pitch it. You also have to consider where you will be fermenting. Garages, basements, sheds, and other uninsulated rooms can fall outside the optimal temperature of many yeasts in winter or summer. The ideal temperature range for most common yeast strains is 65° to 75°F, and it's best to keep it constant through the fermentation. Lager beers are "cold-brewed" as TV commercials claim, with yeasts that perform well at temperatures below 60°F.

An acidic environment—below 4—is ideal for wine yeasts. But ingredients with high acidity, such as honey or tomatoes, can drop the pH to as low as 2. With them, you need a yeast strain that keeps active in the most acidic conditions.

FLOCCULATION. What happens to yeast when it has finished fermenting? The cells begin to clump together. How well the cells clump, when they clump, and where they go after they clump is called flocculation. Wild yeasts don't flocculate well, so the dead cells float around in small aggregates or singly in the fermented liquid, leaving it cloudy and yeasty flavored. The yeasts used in producing most beverages have been chosen for their flocculation, so that the drinks will be clear (or mostly so) when they're done. How this happens is just beginning to be understood, with research published just in the last ten years explaining why yeast strains do this at different rates.

Ideally, yeast will keep fermenting until the drink reaches the final gravity you are aiming for and then the yeast will become flocculent and drop out of the solution. If it happens too soon in the fermentation, your drink will be sweeter than you expected because the yeast will not have consumed enough of the sugar. If it doesn't happen thoroughly or too late in the fermentation, your drink will look cloudy and taste too yeasty.

The goal then is to choose a yeast strain with a flocculation level that matches the drink you want. For ales and stout beers, and some dry ciders—which have a pronounced yeasty flavor and more opaque appearance—yeasts with a low flocculation rating will get you the results you want. Ale yeasts also flocculate to the top, meaning the clumps go to the surface of the wort, rather than to the bottom, as nearly all others do. Yeasts with high flocculation levels are ideal for sparkling wines, meads, and ciders. Most yeasts are characterized as medium flocculation, and are appropriate for a wide range of other drinks.

Temperature and aeration can have a significant effect on yeast's flocculation. Each strain has an ideal temperature at which it forms clumps; when the solution is too warm it can become flocculent too soon, and at low temperatures it may not until too late. Flocculation is generally poor if the yeast does not get enough oxygen. Managing those factors is key to getting your results to match your expectations.

Flocculation is valuable to you for one more reason: the yeast "cake" of flocs in your fermenter can be the yeast you use as a starter to your next batch. To use it, pour the "sludge" at the bottom of the fermenter into a sanitized jar. Boil a few cups of water, let it cool, and pour it into the sludge. An hour later, you'll see it has separated into two layers—sediment on the bottom, a beige slurry of yeast on top. Use it within a few days, while the yeast cells are most active.

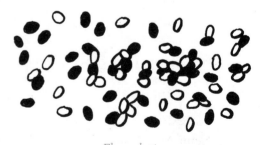

Flocculation

RESULTS. Each strain of yeast produces minute amounts of different compounds while it is in the process of fermenting. How much of each compound it produces depends on the strain's natural tendencies, as well as the ingredients and the conditions it is living in. These compounds—esters, phenols, and ketones primarily—create the wide range of flavors, aromas, and even appearances of fermented drinks. Some promote a smoky taste; others tend to produce flavors from fruity, bitter, and piney to nutty and floral. The many researchers and fermenters who have come before us have found which strains work best to produce the drinks we know and love. When you first start fermenting, sticking with the tried-and-true combinations of yeasts and ingredients teaches you how to get to a specific final result. After you have gained experience and get a sense of how different yeast strains perform, you can have a lot of fun discovering whether you like the results when you create your own combinations.

Yeasts for all kinds of fermenting are available as a dry powder and in liquid. The packets of powder cost less to buy and for shipping, and they're stable, so they tolerate temperature extremes and long (up to a year) storage. But you will find more choices among the liquid yeast products. Liquid yeast does, however, have a shorter shelf life and it is more expensive. The liquids work best when you make a "starter" to initiate their activity (more on that in the next section), while for dry yeasts you need only rehydrate them. Dry yeasts are an easy, affordable option for beginners, but as you gain more experience and want to try different drinks, you'll be turning to the more diverse selection among the liquid yeasts.

⨯⨯⨯⨯⨯⨯⨯⨯⨯⨯⨯⨯⨯⨯ KEEP A JOURNAL ⨯⨯⨯⨯⨯⨯⨯⨯⨯⨯⨯⨯⨯⨯

The old adage goes that you learn from your mistakes, but I've found it's more accurate to say that you learn when you get it right—that is, when you stop making the mistakes. You can only stop making mistakes if you remember what they were. A brewing journal is a crucial tool to help you do just that. Take the time to record every ingredient, every step you take, and most important, the original gravity and each gravity reading along the way, and you will have valuable information that will help you successfully complete the fermentation process each time. And you'll be able to make improvements to your process so that your results get better and better.

PITCHING YEAST

You don't actually throw yeast when you use it, but adding it to your must or wort is referred to as pitching it. I found no reliable explanation as to why people say "pitching," but everybody does. More important than nomenclature, your goal is to put the yeast in the ideal conditions for it to reproduce robustly, feed vigorously, and die gracefully. The steps you take at the very outset of fermentation are critical for the yeast's success in all of these areas.

DRY YEAST. Start to reactivate powdered yeast about twenty minutes before you are ready to pitch it. Get 2 ounces of water for every 5 grams of yeast. The water should be close to, but less than, 104°F. Stir gently, then let stand for about 20 minutes (and not longer than 30 minutes).
The yeast needs to be close to the same temperature (within 10°F) as the must or wort. When the yeast mixture is within the temperature range, stir it gently to distribute the yeast throughout. Pitch it right away.

LIQUID YEAST. For 5 gallons of must or wort, set aside about 16 ounces to be used as a starter for liquid yeast. Pour the starter fluid into a sanitized bottle with cap (a plastic soda bottle works) and then add the liquid yeast (you may need a sanitized funnel for this). Seal with the cap and shake to stir. In twelve to eighteen hours, the yeast will be through—or mostly through—its lag period and will be raring to go when you pitch it. Some brands of yeast now come in "smack" packs. With those, the starter is included and you simply break the seal between the yeast and starter with a light smack about twelve hours before you pitch it.

✕✕✕✕✕✕✕✕✕BOOTLEGGER OR HOME BREWER? ✕✕✕✕✕✕✕✕✕

Federal law allows you to make 100 gallons of wine per year for one person, 200 gallons annually for a household. You can sell alcoholic beverages or distill them only with permits from your state. Two hundred gallons amounts to one thousand 750 ml bottles. Five gallons of wine equals twenty-five average-size bottles.

✕✕✕✕✕✕✕✕✕✕ FERMENTATION STEPS ✕✕✕✕✕✕✕✕✕✕

Each type of fermentation has its own unique components, and I'll explain those in the chapters focused on the specific drinks. But right here, all in one place, I want to share a few basics that apply to all alcohol fermentation.

SANITIZE EVERYTHING. Thoroughly cleaning, drying, and sanitizing all of your gear is always the first and last step in the process. This is critically important, but I promise I won't harp on it any further. If you don't understand why it is so important or how to do it properly, please see page 20.

PREPARE YOUR INGREDIENTS. Once you've gathered your ingredients, work quickly but carefully to get them ready for fermentation. That is, crush the fruit, heat the honey, sprout and mash the grain, and boil the wort. When your must or wort is ready, take a hydrometer reading. This will be the original gravity.

SITE THE BUCKET. Put your primary fermentation bucket in a cool, dry place away from direct sunlight. Ideally, you have a spot for it on a low shelf where it can sit undisturbed for several weeks.

START THE YEAST. Activate your yeast, either by rehydrating it or making a starter for it.

BLEND IN ADDITIVES. If you are using sulfites to add stability and protect against bacteria, add them to your must. Mix in any other additives you are using, such as yeast nutrient, tannins, or pectic enzyme.

PITCH THE YEAST. The yeast needs oxygen at this stage, so there are some experts who advocate leaving the lid off the bucket for the first few days, whereas others believe putting the lid on ensures that no debris or pests land in it. If you choose to put the lid on, gently stir the must or wort every twelve hours or so for the first few days to introduce oxygen into it.

LOOK FOR BUBBLES. The liquid begins bubbling in as little as two days and may take up to five days until the yeast shifts from its reproductive state to full-strength sugar conversion.

SET THE LOCK. When the bubbling begins, put on the bucket's lid and attach the airlock. The lock will have a cup in which you put fluid that acts as a barrier to airborne bacteria. You can use distilled water or vodka in the cup—vodka is most effective, but it evaporates faster than water.

MAKE NOTES. Keeping a detailed journal is a very valuable tool for ensuring that your current batch turns out the way you expect it to and helps you learn from mistakes. Take the time early in your process to record all of the ingredients you've used and the original gravity of your must or wort. Also note how long you waited for the bubbling to start and when it peaks.

CHECK DAILY. While the yeast is at its peak of producing alcohol, you'll see a steady flow of bubbles in the airlock, showing you that carbon dioxide is being released. The bubbling will gradually slow to just a few each minute. If you smell rotten eggs, you can "take the wine for a walk" by aerating it, either by stirring it or racking it into an open container and back—then add more nitrogen or yeast food.

RACK IT. When the vigorous bubbling of primary fermentation has slowed, you are ready to "rack" the drink. The process of racking is the transfer of the fluid from the primary fermenter to a vessel, typically a glass carboy, for a longer, slower secondary fermentation. During this period, the surviving yeast consumes unwanted compounds, helping to smooth the drink's flavor, while the dead yeast flocculates and settles to the bottom.

Transferring the fluid from one container to another requires plastic tubing and is made much easier with a siphon pump. I suggested a few paragraphs back that you put your fermentation bucket on a shelf not only because it will be out of the way, but also because it sets you up for gravity to help you get the flow going when the secondary container is lower than the first. If you don't have it on a shelf, you can just put the primary bucket on a table or sturdy chair. Move the bucket a day or at least several hours before you are ready to rack it, to allow time for the sediment to resettle in the bucket after you've sloshed it around while lifting it.

If you are working without a racking cane, keep the tubing a few inches above the bottom of the bucket so that you don't get sediment in the tube and transfer it to the new container.

TAKE ANOTHER READING. With your hydrometer, check the gravity of your must or wort when you rack it. Compare the measurement to the original gravity. As the ingredients were processed into alcohol, the gravity decreases (because alcohol is lighter than water). At the first racking, you should note a significant decline in the gravity reading. The change will gradually slow and when your readings are the same for several weeks, you'll know that the fermentation has just about ceased. If you don't want the drink to change further, you can simply add sulfites to kill off any remaining yeast or chill it to below 40°F. If you can wait, the lingering yeast will continue to clarify and mellow the flavor as your wine, cider, or mead ages.

If you want a sparkling or carbonated drink, you want to leave those last yeast cells alive and hungry so they can produce a little more bubbly carbon dioxide for you in the bottle. I'll get to that in a moment.

ACID CHANGE. Wines made from grapes can develop high levels of malic acid, which has a sharp taste that overwhelms other flavors. Makers of fine red wines (and some whites) use natural bacterias to transform malic acid into softer, almost buttery lactic acid. This "malolactic" fermentation, stimulated by inoculants available from wine suppliers, takes about two months after the yeast fermentation is over. Malolactic fermentation adds complexity to the flavor of sophisticated wines, but it also reduces fruitiness in the taste. Be aware that the bacteria that converts malic to lactic acid also turns citric acid (as is found in lemon juice) into acetic acid, commonly known as vinegar. If you decide to try malolactic fermentation with your wine, use packaged acid blends or tartaric acid, rather than lemon juice, to reduce the pH of your must.

BOTTLE WHEN READY. A day or two before you are ready to bottle, move the carboy you've used for secondary fermentation to a spot a few feet off the ground. Rack the drink once more, but this time into your primary fermentation bucket or another one you've cleaned, sanitized, and readied as a bottling container. Bring along as little sediment as possible, even if it costs you an ounce or two of drink that gets left behind. Ideally, your bottling container is also set a couple of feet higher than the ground.

A bottle filler with built-in shutoff valve helps limit spilling and overflows, but you can fill bottles with a funnel and simple (and sanitized) plastic tubing. Whether you use new or used bottles, be sure to clean and sanitize them well first, and allow them to dry completely.

As you fill the bottles, leave no more than $1/2$ inch of headspace below the lid. Too much space will expose your drink to oxygen, which can alter the flavor, odor, and color. Be sure to seal the bottles completely, you don't want oxygen getting to the drink.

PRIME FOR CARBONATION. Commercial brewers and sparkling winemakers typically inject carbon dioxide into the fluid to create the bubbles you enjoy when you open them. But at home you can stimulate yeast to produce CO_2 for you the way it is done in champagne by feeding them a little more sugar when you bottle but not enough to generate much additional alcohol. Dissolve about $1/2$ cup of sugar or honey (if you're making mead) in 16 ounces of water and add that to 5 gallons of must or wort fluid before you bottle. The remaining yeast will make just enough carbon dioxide to bubble up your drink without creating so much pressure the lids blow. The carbonation process takes at least two weeks. Store the bottles in a place where they will do no harm if they do pop and you can keep an eye on them.

AGING GRACEFULLY. Many wines as well as mead and cider may still have raw flavors even when you bottle them. Over time, natural processes continue to smooth out the flavor. This can take as little as six months for cider, but for most wines and meads you want to wait at least a year before you drink them, to get their peak of flavor. Patience is a virtue, though I understand it's not an easy one to master. When you do finally drink your homemade wine, you'll be glad you waited. You need not wait as long to enjoy the beer you brew—it's ready to drink when the carbonation peaks.

Winemakers and brewers discovered centuries ago that oak barrels impart tannins and other desirable flavor components to drinks stored in them. Even if you don't have room for oak barrels where you live, you can get the flavor by using oak chips or powder during fermentation. You can find different "flavors" of chips and powders, created by toasting and seasoning the wood in a variety of ways. If you're sure of how much oak flavor you want, you can add it during primary fermentation—the first week or two. In that case, use oak powder, at a rate of about one-third of an ounce per gallon (for white and light fruit wines and mead) to 1/2 ounce of oak powder per gallon of red wines and heavier fruit and vegetable wines. Adding oak flavor with chips during the secondary fermentation is easier to manage since you can strain out the oak chips as soon as you've hit the flavor you want. A half-ounce to an ounce of chips per gallon is a moderate amount to begin testing how much oak flavor you like. Leave the chips in the fluid for about a week—after that, the oak may start to dominate other flavor components. You can also oak a portion of the wine and blend it back, for better control.

KEY TERMS

ABV. Alcohol by volume, or ABV, is the percentage of alcohol in the drink, and indicates how potent it will be. You can calculate the ABV by subtracting the final gravity (FG) reading from the original gravity (OG) and multiplying by 131.
An example: OG = 1.070, FG = 0.998. 1.070 − 0.998 = 0.072. ABV=9.4 percent.

AUTOLYSIS. This is the process of yeast breaking down the sediment in a fermentation vessel. It can leave behind unwanted flavors.

BENTONITE. Clay used for clarifying a wine. It's made of tiny fossils that carry a charge, attracting proteins and sediments and precipitating them out.

BALLING/BRIX. The measurement on a refractometer that calculates the sugar content of a liquid.

CAP. The pulp and skins that float to the top of the must during the early stages of fermentation. To punch the cap means to remix the floating debris with the liquid.

FINING. The process of clearing out pulp and other sediment left floating in wine, while reducing astringency, bitterness, and off-odors. A variety of products are available for this, including Bentonite and Chitosan.

LEES. The dead yeast that forms a kind of sludge or cake at the bottom of a fermentation vessel. Makers of white wines may keep it "on the lees" after fermenting, because it improves the taste and mouthfeel of the wines.

MUST. The blend of ingredients, including juice, pulp, and skins, or honey before fermentation turns it into wine, mead, or cider.

PITCH YEAST. Adding yeast to must or wort. No one seems to have a definitive answer about why it's known as pitching yeast, but everyone refers to it that way.

RACKING. Siphoning clear liquid from one container to another to take it away from the lees and other sediment in a carboy.

WORT. The blend of water, grains, and hops—along with any other added ingredients—that is transformed by fermentation into beer.

XX

CHAPTER № 2

HOMEGROWN WINES

THE RAW INGREDIENTS FOR GREAT WINE ARE EASY FOR YOU TO GROW, even if you don't live in the south of France or Northern California. Your yard, even a small one, can produce fruits and vegetables for making wines that capture and enhance their flavors. In this chapter, we'll cover a wide variety of ingredients, including grapes, berries, tree fruits, vegetables, and a few foraged foods that you can try even if you have no place to grow anything. "Country wines"—made from what you grow—may not have the complex, nuanced flavors of the finely crafted vintages produced with the best-known grape varietals, but they do capture the taste of fresh air, sunshine, and real ingredients. Grapes are a reliable place to start making wine, but I hope you'll be inspired to consider trying other raw materials. You'll find information here on how to grow and prepare the variety of ingredients for making wine, and specifics on using them to make wine. I've started with the most common and easiest ingredient for making wine—grapes—and then continue in that order of most to least common.

For an overview of how fermentation transforms them into alcohol and the steps involved, check out Chapter 1, "Fermentation Basics." But before we dig into the specifics for the ingredients, it will be helpful to get into a few details for making wine with any of them.

XXXXXXXXXXXXXXXXXXXXXXXXXXXXXXXXXXXXXXXX

FLAVOR EXTRACTION. To enjoy the taste of homegrown ingredients in your wine, you need to get their sugars and flavor components into your must. That's simple enough with grapes, blueberries, and other soft fruits. You squeeze them to burst their skins and release the juices into your primary bucket. You want to avoid crushing the seeds and stems into the fruit—their bitterness can overpower other flavors. A wine with balanced flavors needs the bitter bite of tannins that are found in grapes and a few other kinds of fruit. For ingredients with no natural tannins, you can use strong black tea or commercial tannin blends to add the flavor to your must.

When making red wine with grapes, leaving the skins in the must deepens the flavor and adds color. Berries have lots of tiny seeds that you want to keep out of your must. To do that, put the fruit in a nylon bag or a cheesecloth (that you don't mind getting stained) and crush the fruit in the bag over your bucket. After adding water to the juice (so that you have 1 gallon of fluid), steep the bag of fruit in the must for twenty-four hours before you get it ready for fermentation. Squeeze the bag once more over the bucket before you discard the contents in your compost pile.

Ingredients that are less juicy need a more active approach to extracting their flavor. For pulpy tree fruits and vegetables, begin by slicing them, removing their seeds, and crushing the fruit to release as much juice as you can. Then pour a gallon of boiling water over the crushed fruit to capture more of its flavor into liquid form. Let the fruit steep in the water for a few hours before straining it out and getting the must ready to ferment. Hot water also is the best way to get the flavor from hard root vegetables and delicate flowers, such as dandelions, but both of them need to simmer in a large stock-pot for thirty minutes (flowers) to sixty minutes (roots). Put the ingredients in the pot after a gallon of water comes to a boil and then has cooled back to a slow, steady simmer. Keep the lid on to keep volatile flavor compounds inside the pot. After straining the water into the fermentation bucket, you can extract a bit more flavor by squeezing a bag full of the remaining pulp into the must.

SWEET STUFF. Sugar, you should recall, is the food of yeast. Grape juice has a high sugar concentration—enough, in most cases, to make a potent wine without supplemental sweetener. But few other fruits or vegetables have enough of their own sugar to produce wine that's stronger than weak cider, so you need to add sweetener to those types of musts. Granulated table sugar is the most common choice because it's manufactured to dissolve evenly and leave behind no taste other than sweet. Powdered sugar will cloud your wine, which you don't want, and brown sugar alters the flavor, which you may want with a few but not all wines. You can use honey, but it, too, has its own flavor; it's better used to make mead, or honey wine (more about that on page 140). Many makers of "country wines," as these unique, handcrafted drinks are often called, use chopped raisins to sweeten their musts. Whichever type of sugar you go with, be sure it is thoroughly blended in before you take the hydrometer reading to determine the starting gravity.

The only sugar you will add after fermentation is priming sugar, used to create a sparkling wine. The same types of sugar that are used in the must work for priming, too, or you can buy specialized priming sugar (made from corn). Before you bottle your wine, dissolve the sugar in water ($^1/_2$ cup of sugar to 1 cup of water for a gallon of wine) and pour it into your carboy or bottling bucket. Add a half-packet (about 5 grams or 0.20 ounces) of fresh yeast to the wine (no nutrients needed in this case). The yeast will be stimulated to feed and produce carbon dioxide, the natural pop in your bubbly, but very little additional alcohol.

TOPPED OFF. The main ingredient in wine is water. I covered which type of water works best on page 21, so here I just want to address the need to add it continually to the wine during the process. You add it to the must to get your fluid level up to the amount of wine you're planning to make. Each time you rack the wine, you lose a little fluid. You also may lose some to evaporation over time.

Adding water to make up the difference is important because after the early stages of fermentation, exposure to oxygen can ruin your wine's flavor and color. To prevent oxidation, you need to limit the amount of air that comes in contact with the wine. The way to do this is keep carboys and bottles filled to within $^1/_2$ inch of their opening at all times. Most home vintners use water for topping off, but when it's a small amount that you need to add, you can also top off with a little wine from a similar, prior batch. If you do use water, you may want to make wine with a slightly higher alcohol concentration than you want to finish with because you will be diluting a bit along the way.

OXYGEN IN AND OUT. At the start of fermentation, the yeast needs access to oxygen. As you may recall from the basic steps of fermentation (page 35), you introduce oxygen into your must with vigorous stirring. And for the first few days, you keep the must in an open bucket (covered only with a cheesecloth) so that the yeast can continue to get oxygen from the air.

But as soon as the primary fermentation has slowed—when the interval between bubbles is five minutes or more—the wine has to be isolated from air. That's the time to transfer it to a carboy with an airlock. Try to limit splashing the must as you transfer it, as splashing introduces oxygen—pour it down the sides of the carboy, if possible.

During this first transfer, you want to strain out any pulp or other fruit debris that is left in the must, but you don't want to remove the yeast, so include all of the lees (floating clumps of yeast) to continue the fermentation in the secondary fermenter, or carboy. Be sure to fill it to within $\frac{1}{2}$ inch of the top and set up the airlock right away.

RACKING WINE. Transferring wine from one container to another, known as racking it, is a critical step in producing a clean, fresh-tasting drink. You can rack at regular intervals, such as thirty, forty, or sixty days, but you don't need to be tied to specific time schedule. However, leave at least three weeks between each racking so you don't expose the wine to air too often. Be sure to rack at least every ninety days, as rotting yeast can produce off-flavors in the wine. As long as you see fresh yeast deposits—the "lees" in the bottom of carboy, you want to continue to rack it. When you don't see any new deposits for thirty days, the wine is ready for bottling.

BOUND FOR BOTTLES. Before you bottle wine, you want to be sure the fermentation has completely ceased (except in the case of sparkling wine). Wines with a final gravity below 0.990, the driest wines, are finished fermenting because there is too little sugar for the yeast to continue feeding. Wines with more sugar need to be stabilized—by killing the remaining yeast—to stop fermentation. You can stabilize wine with cold or with chemicals. If you can keep the wine cooler than 32°F (but not so cold it freezes) for three to four weeks, you can be sure the yeast is gone. If you can't keep the wine consistently cold, potassium sorbate, a compound sold as Sorbistat K, works, too. Use about $\frac{1}{2}$ teaspoon per gallon of wine.

When bottling, leave $\frac{1}{4}$ inch between the top of the wine and the bottom of the cork. Let the bottles stand for three days after filling to allow it to further settle, then store the bottles on their side with the wine in contact with the cork.

GRAPES

People have been making wine from grapes for all of recorded history and even back before that, and have been using it as a sacrament, intoxicant, and accompaniment to food ever since. As you'll see in this chapter, you can make wine from many fruits and even vegetables, herbs, and wild plants. So why, you might wonder, did grapes become the fruit most commonly made into wine? They are exceptionally high in sugar balanced by both acidity and astringency, and their skins naturally host yeasts that will turn those sugars into alcohol. You can imagine early people leaving a bowl of juice, pulp, and skins in a container for a week or two and discovering wine almost by accident.

You are most likely to start making your own wine with grapes because they're easiest to ferment—they have all the sugars, acids, tannins, and other flavor components already, so you don't need to add any ingredients except water and yeast. And you already know what grape wine is supposed to taste like. You don't have to live in one of the world's great wine-producing regions to grow grapes. They're adapted to the many climates and soils of North America and they can be planted in a small urban plot, as well as areas with more land. Grapevines take some initial effort, but once established they're easy to manage. You could also forage for wild grapes, which grow in uncultivated areas in cities and suburbs as well as rural areas, and use them to make wine.

Growing your own grapes to make wine not only gives you a personal *terroir*—okay, maybe not one that will rival Bordeaux or Napa—it also gives you the smoother tasting first pressing, or free run, juice rather than the lower-quality second and third pressings, which are the main ingredient in most "table wines" and other blends. You can also be sure the grapes you've raised are organic and the wine is made with the purest ingredients.

VARIETALS

The more than five thousand grape varieties belong to two species. *Vitis vinifera* includes all types of the European wine grapes, such as Merlot, Chardonnay, and Pinot Noir. They are very well adapted to the conditions around the Mediterranean and in the Pacific Northwest of the United States, where the world's best-known vineyards are. *Vitis labrusca*, sometimes called fox grapes, are native to North America, so they're better adapted to the conditions in most of the United States. Concord and Catawba have long been the two best-known varietals. If you like simple wine with a pronounced grape flavor and a light tinge of alcohol, you will be able to make plenty of it with either (or both) of those two very productive varieties.

Hybrids bearing the finer flavor of the Europeans with the hardier growing habits of the fox grapes are now available and widely grown throughout the United States. Unless you live in one of the ideal wine-growing areas, the hybrids are your best bet, though many growers in other regions with the perfect microclimate buck the odds and succeed with the European types.

If you'd like to make red wine with deep, bold flavor, the hybrid Chambourcin has been the main ingredient in many award winners. It is higher in the key flavor component, tannins, than most other hybrid varieties. The fruit matures late in the season—no doubt, one reason why the wines made with it taste so full bodied. But it may ripen too late for growers where frost comes early in the fall. Marechal Foch is a reliable producer in even very cold climates, and the wines it yields are nearly as rich tasting.

For new grape growers, Cayuga White is a reliable choice. It is very disease resistant and highly productive. Its fruit is both very sweet and acidic, so it works well for both dry and dessert wines. Vidal Blanc is also productive, but it is not as hardy as Cayuga White. Vidal Blanc works very well in dry wines, but for the most sophisticated flavor from a hybrid white grape, you want Seyval Blanc. Its flavor reminds some tasters of Riesling. To make sweet white wine that still has a distinct acidity, plant Vignoles, which fares best where frost comes late in the season.

Growing several different varieties both increases your chances for success—if one variety turns out not to be well adapted to your conditions, you won't be left with no fruit—and gives you different flavor profiles to work with. Unlike many other fruits, grapes are self-pollinating, so you do not need to plant more than one variety or even more than one vine for it to produce a hefty harvest for you. You need not worry, however, about their cross-pollinating. You can plant a red wine grapevine next to a white wine grapevine and each will reliably bear its own type of fruit.

SITE

No matter which variety you plant, sunlight and air circulation are your top priorities for growing healthy, hassle-free grapes. The vines grow best where they get ten or more hours of direct sun during the summer. If you live where summers are humid, morning sun is best—the light dries off the dew early in the day, suppressing unpleasant diseases and fungi from forming on the fruit. Plant the vines far enough away from buildings, fences, trees, and shrubs so that breezes can circulate in and around them. Vineyards are typically planted on slopes for the same reason—colder, damper air settles at the bottom of slopes, keeping the vines warmer, drier, and cleaner. Planting grapes where they get morning sun and plenty of air flow are the most valuable steps you can take to ensure you get clean and fresh-tasting fruit and wine.

If you have about 3 square feet of ground, you can grow a grapevine in it. Unlike many other fruits, grapes are not easily managed in containers. They need to be able to spread out their vines and be trained to grow up a trellis. Still, you don't need a lot of ground area for them. I have seen grapes growing well in the tiny lots behind row houses and other spots where space is very limited.

Grapevine Training

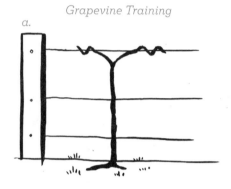
a.

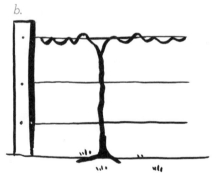
b.

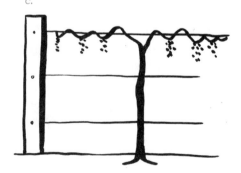
c.

SOIL

Grapes grow in thin soils with low fertility. The soil does need to be well drained, however, because grape vines suffer problems when their roots sit in standing water. Another reason why planting on a slope is ideal: Water drains away from the roots. Sandy soil is low in fertility and well drained. If you have sandy soil, simply work in compost to provide nutrients and help the soil disperse moisture evenly. Where the soil is predominantly clay, loosen the soil as far down as you can, to a foot or more if possible. Also mix in a lot of compost or other organic matter (e.g., dried leaves, grass clippings, or peat) to help keep it loose and allow water and nutrients to reach the roots.

Resist the urge to add fertilizer (especially the synthetic kind) to the soil so your grape vines grow big quickly. Grape roots are vulnerable to soil-borne diseases that flourish in high-nitrogen soils, such as those saturated in fertilizer.

PLANTING

A grape vine produces on average 15 to 20 pounds of fruit each season or enough for 5 gallons of wine. Depending on the conditions, some seasons you will get more fruit, others less.

Early spring, as soon as the soil temperatures is consistently warmer than 45°F, is the best time to plant grape vines. If you live where winter temperatures don't come too early, you can also plant in late summer to early fall.

After soaking the vines overnight in buckets of water, dig a hole that's 2 feet deep and wide. At the bottom, form a small mound of soil and spread the vines' roots out over it. Gently backfill the hole with a mixture of the soil you dug out and organic matter. Firm the soil around the vine with your hands, but don't press it so hard you squeeze all the air out. Water the soil and be sure it stays consistently moist until you see new growth on top, typically two to three weeks after you've transplanted the vines to your yard.

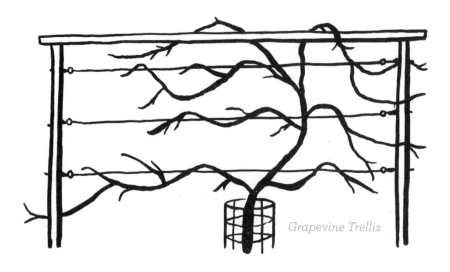

Grapevine Trellis

CARE

You'll harvest your own grapes two seasons after you plant the vines. In the meantime, your primary responsibility is to train them—not to roll over or fetch, but to sit up on a trellis and grow over it. A trellis is as simple as three posts with wires stretched between them but can also be a more elaborate arbor or just a split-rail fence. The roots are planted between the posts and the vines are tied to the wires or rails so they grow in different directions from each other. Vineyards that want to maximize productivity tend to use the cordon training system, training a pair of canes—fruiting vines that branch off of the main central trunk—to grow vertically along wires.

Whatever you use to hold up your grapevines, remember that you need to prune them annually (ideally in late winter) to remove old canes that are passed their fruiting

stage and to allow room for fresh new shoots that will bear future crops for you. You also want to prune off canes that overlap with your four primary vines to allow for that all-important air circulation.

After your grapevines are established—that is, they're growing leaves and new shoots—you don't need to water them except during very long, hot, and dry spells. Spreading an inch or two of compost around the base of them after the annual harvest is all the feeding they need. Steady airflow and well-drained soil keep diseases and fungi to a minimum. But there are pests, particularly Japanese beetles in the eastern half of the United States, and scale, a nearly transparent and immobile insect that suffocates the vine.

Keep a birdbath near your grapevines and your feathered friends will munch many of these pests for you. You can handpick the bugs and drop them in a bucket of soapy water. Insecticidal soap spray, an organic pest control that's not harmful to people, pets, or wildlife except insects, is also an effective way to protect your grape harvest from pests.

HARVEST

All grapes begin as small, hard, dark green berries. In late summer, they begin to swell as they fill with juice and then ripen to their final color. White varieties turn more golden and their skins get a glossy shine. Red wine grapes darken and develop a dusky coating on their skins. The leaves on the vines are also changing colors, yellow or reddish, as the grapes reach their peak of ripeness. Most important, their concentration of sugars spikes and acids decline.

Versaison is the term experienced vintners use to describe the time between when the grapes begin to change color and when they are fully ripe. It is a period when world-class wine grape producers pay careful attention to their crop. Picked too late, the grapes will be too sweet and carry the flavor of decay. Picked too early, the grapes will be too acidic and taste too vegetal. The weather and other variables affect the exact best time to harvest each growing season.

Tasting a few of your grapes as they ripen trains your palate to recognize when the sugars and acids reach a balance. A refractometer helps you know for sure when they're ready. To test your crop, crush a few handfuls in a large bowl and strain the juice. The sugar density should be around 22° Brix, or 1.0982 specific gravity (SG), producing a wine that's up to 11 percent alcohol. You want to be sure you wait until the grapes are fully ripe because their flavor does not improve after you harvest them.

When the grapes are ready, use sharp pruners or shears to clip the clusters from the vines. Try to pick a day and time when the grapes are driest. Wooden crates are the best storage vessels, but plastic trays work fine, too. Avoid stacking the grapes in many layers, to keep from damaging those at the bottom. Store them in a cool, dry spot for a few days so they can dry off.

MAKING WINE

AMOUNT OF FRUIT (for 5 gallons of wine): 20 pounds

ADDITIONAL INGREDIENTS: Water

PREPARATION: Put the fruit in a bucket and gently crush it to cause the juice to burst out of the skin. You can use a plate, your hands, or the time-honored bare foot, if the bucket fits. (It should go without saying that your foot must be thoroughly clean.) Don't grind the grapes into a pulp or you'll crush the seeds, which leaves behind a bitter taste in the wine.

For red wine, leave the skins in the must during fermentation. For white, remove the skins as soon as the grapes are crushed. Red or white, be sure to strain out stems and seeds. After straining the juice into the fermentation bucket, add enough water to get to 5 gallons, stir well and cover lightly, then wait forty-eight hours to pitch the yeast.

BEST YEAST: Montrachet Red or White
TIME TO DRINK: One year or more

✕✕✕✕✕✕✕✕✕✕✕✕✕✕✕✕ SPOTLIGHT ON: ✕✕✕✕✕✕✕✕✕✕✕✕✕✕✕✕
CARDINAL HOLLOW WINERY, NORTH WALES, PENNSYLVANIA

IN THE 1990s, CHRISTOPHER BOYD TRAVELED FREQUENTLY FOR HIS JOB AND discovered a taste for fine wine at the high-end restaurants he dined at with clients. "With time on my hands on planes, I started reading about wine," Boyd recalls. "First, I was learning more about the different wines and how to choose them, but before long my interest led me to making it."

Boyd began by making a 1-gallon batch of Concord grape wine and soon switched to 5-gallon batches. After tasting raspberry mead that a friend made, he sought other challenges for himself. "I tried making Cabernets, Gewürztraminers, and other fine wines, and while I was pleased with the results I also wanted to make something different, something that you don't find at every store. I made strawberry wine and it had a distinct real strawberry scent and a light strawberry flavor, but it still tasted like wine," he says. After his garden yielded a large crop of jalapeños one summer, he decided to try making wine with it. He liked the wine and so did friends and family, and he followed his tastes to try more ingredients. After years of sharing his homemade wines, Boyd decided in 2008 to turn his hobby into a business. Today, he offers his customers twenty-five different kinds of wine, including traditional reds and whites, as well as those made with dandelions, watermelon, and elderberries, and several kinds of mead. Boyd's wines have won awards at national competitions and he operates five tasting rooms in the Philadelphia metropolitan area. "I'm up to fifty-gallon batches now—I'm averaging about two thousand gallons a year," he says, "but the keys are the same no matter how much I am making.

"I follow a recipe once," he continues, "after that I begin to tinker with it to make it my own. With grapes, the variables are minimal, because you are only working with grapes and yeast. You can vary the blend of grapes you use, the type of yeast, and the aging period, but not much more. When you work with other kinds of fruit, you have a lot more to play with—your must is not just juice, but a brew of different flavors and active ingredients."

Boyd emphasizes that making wine can seem like guesswork, but that over time you will discover what he calls "repeatable flavors" in your wine. With experience, these become your guideposts. "Sample your wine at every stage in the process, starting with the raw must and at every racking," Boyd advises. "You're tasting for sweetness, bitterness, and acids, and for the flavor components of the fruit. The balance between them evolves as the wine ferments and ages, but you want to taste them all at each stage. As you get more experience with an ingredient or a blend, you will develop your sense of what the balance needs to be to get the results you want. You'll never know exactly how a wine will turn out when you taste it at the start, but you can get a reliable idea of whether it will taste good."

This trained sense of taste and how to anticipate the results are the true secret to success in making wine with any ingredient, Boyd says. "Making wine requires a basic knowledge of the science involved, but it is most of all an art," he concludes. "You can be taught the fundamentals of the process, but no one can teach you the art. You have to learn that yourself by trial and error."

You can see all of Boyd's products, place an order for them, and find out when you can visit his tasting rooms at www.cardinalhollowwinery.com.

✕✕✕✕✕✕✕✕✕✕✕✕✕✕ BERRIES ✕✕✕✕✕✕✕✕✕✕✕✕✕✕✕✕

Grapes are actually berries, but they're not the only berries for making wine. Raspberries, blackberries, and blueberries could not be easier to grow—they grow wild in many of the remaining unpaved and uncultivated areas of North America. Strawberries take a bit more effort to grow and gooseberries and currants are less common. All of them produce wines that capture the balance of sweetness, tartness, and acidity that is unique to each type of berry.

VARIETALS

BLUEBERRIES give you choices based on your climate. In the Northeast and Midwest, highbush blueberries are native, and handle the cold winters and humid summers well. Coville is a highbush that bears big, juicy berries that have a particularly tart taste, an appealing quality for fruit you want to make into wine. Where winters are frigid, lowbush blueberries can survive from one season to the next. Burgundy and Claret are lowbush varieties, though they've been named more for their color than because they taste like wine grapes. Tophat is a very compact lowbush plant that can be grown in a small space or even a container. Rabbiteye varieties do not need the chilling hours (winter temperatures below freezing) that the other types must have to renew themselves each year, and they ripen their berries before summer heat sets in. For those reasons, they're the best choice in the South. Premier is a very productive rabbiteye variety with plump, juicy fruit on a shrub that stays moderately sized. Bear in mind that most blueberry varieties need to be planted with another variety to pollinate them, so you'll need to choose at least two types.

RASPBERRIES are one crop every garden should have. You can plant them in your poorest soil (as long as it's a sunny spot) and they will flourish for years. They do spread, but not as aggressively as blackberries, and the canes are not as thorny, so they're easier to manage. The berries are very sweet with a hint of acidity, and they impart those appealing flavors to wine, meads, and infusions. When choosing a variety, you will see yellow, purple/black, and red options. The yellow and purple/black raspberries are delicious and rarely found in stores, but they are not as productive as the more common red types. They may be either ever-bearing types or summer-bearing. The former produce two modest crops a year—in late spring and in fall. For a heavier yield that comes all at once—most convenient for making wine—get summer-bearing raspberries. Meeker yields medium-size, juicy berries with a high sugar content. Willamette's berries are bigger and lower in sugar, so they have a tarter taste. Raspberries are self-fruitful, meaning you don't have to plant two different varieties to pollinate each other.

BLACKBERRIES come in three basic types: trailing, erect, and semierect. The trailing types are native to the Pacific Northwest and grow wild there. You need lots of room to grow them because the canes run along the ground and can reach up to 20 feet long. Among those, Marion (sometimes sold as marionberry) is renowned for its sweet flavor. In most other climates, erect or semierect types are a better choice. They're more winter hardy and take up less room—at least initially. All blackberries are fast spreaders, colonizing available space almost overnight. Navaho is a good choice for planting in a garden because it's a little less aggressive, the canes are thornless, and the medium-size fruit are flavorful and not overly seedy.

STRAWBERRIES may produce all of their fruit in just a few weeks in June (so-called June-bearers), give you modest harvests in spring and late summer (known as ever-bearing), or yield a handful of berries each week over the whole summer (these are day-neutral). The June-bearing varieties are the best choice for growing strawberries to make wine. You may have noticed that commercially grown strawberries—like you find in supermarkets and salad bars just about all year long—have been bred for size and shelf life rather than for flavor. They're also typically picked before they're ripe so they can survive the long trip from the warm climates where they're grown. Commercial strawberries have been found to have half as much sugar as those fully ripened on the vine. Growing your own ensures that you can grow varieties that taste best and have the most real fruit sugar, reducing the need to add processed sugar when making wine with them. Jewel is a taste-test winner among the June-bearers, and Honeoye has a noticeably honey-sweet taste that will make for flavorful wine.

Gooseberries and currants used to be planted at nearly every homestead and farm. My German-immigrant grandparents grew them in their tiny city backyard in Philadelphia. But nowadays you don't see them often and many people don't even know what they are. That's partly because some states have bans on planting them—they once were believed to carry viruses destructive to other species. Most of those bans have now been repealed, but these fruits have fallen out of favor because there is little or no commercial market for them. Gooseberries are like small, juicy grapes with a pronounced tart flavor. Of the two available types, European and American, the former taste better and bear larger fruit, but the latter are better adapted to conditions in North America. Poorman is an American type that bears plump, tart yellow-green berries. Invicta is the best-known and most widely available European variety. Currants are even smaller, almost the size of Tic Tac breath mints, and their flavor is more tart. You can choose from red, black, and yellow varieties. Red is most widely adapted, but the black is most prized for its flavor, which is used to make the sweet liqueur crème de cassis. Rovada is a hardy, productive red variety, White Imperial is a tasty yellow, and Crusader bears juicy black fruit.

SITE

All berries are most productive in bright, sunny spots where the soil is not usually soggy. The best site allows air to flow around the plants from all directions, protecting the fruit from fungal diseases.

You can grow strawberries and currants in a small garden or even in containers, but to get a harvest hefty enough to make wine, berries need room to grow and spread. For strawberries, gooseberries, and currants, one or two 4-by-10-foot beds is enough room. Raspberries need a bit more room so they can spread and renew themselves each year. Blueberries require at least enough room to plant more than one shrub, which can reach 8 or more feet in diameter when fully mature. Blackberries quickly become a hedge—and a prickly one that can be very effective at keeping unwanted pests (people and wildlife) out of your garden—and need a lot of room to spread. Yards of room.

SOIL

Blackberries, blueberries, raspberries, gooseberries, and currants grow well in soil that's low in fertility and would be not hospitable to most other food crops. They do need good drainage—the plants may survive in a spot where water collects regularly, but the fruit will be prone to mold and other problems with fungi. These berry bushes, especially blueberries, grow and produce best where the soil is acidic. Just about everywhere in North America except the Southwest, the soil tends to be naturally acidic. You can help keep the pH in the acidic range (below 7) by adding leaves and needles from evergreens to the soil before you plant and by using those materials as mulch while the plants are becoming established. If, however, you live where the soil is naturally alkaline, no amount of soil amending will change it—you need to choose other crops to grow.

Strawberries can grow in low-fertility soil, but they fare better with more nutrients. Prep your strawberry bed by mixing compost into the soil before you plant and spread a $1/2$-inch or so layer of compost around each one twice a year—in early spring before they start producing flowers and berries and again after they've finished bearing fruit for the season.

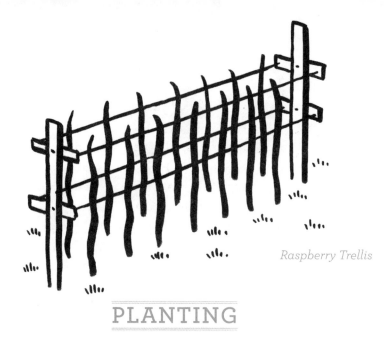

Raspberry Trellis

PLANTING

Blackberry and raspberry canes each bear a quart or two of fruit each season. To make 5 gallons of wine, you need about 20 pounds of berries. A quart of blackberries weighs about a pound, so you need about 20 productive canes to get enough fruit for a batch of wine. Blackberries and raspberries start producing fruit in their first year after planting, but reach their peak about three years after you put them in.

Blueberries, gooseberries, and currants bear little if any fruit for three years after planting, but when they reach maturity, each shrub yields as much as 9 pounds in an average growing season, or about half as much as you need to make 5 gallons of wine. Remember that nearly all blueberry varieties need at least two different kinds planted within a few feet of each other to be thoroughly pollinated and to produce a full flush of fruit.

Early spring, about four weeks before the average last frost date in your area, and early fall, at least four weeks before the average first frost date in your area, are the best times to plant blackberries, raspberries blueberries, gooseberries, and currants. Commercial growers plant in rows to make it easy for them to use machines to cultivate and harvest the crop. In home gardens you don't need to plant in rows, but if you want to maximize your harvest, setting up rows of blackberry and raspberry plants makes it easier to get them to grow on a trellis made of posts and wires, which keeps the canes upright and the fruit more accessible to you. If you plant these shrubs in a row, leave about 3 feet between each individual and 6 feet between each row.

You will be planting crowns, or clumps of roots attached to one main stem. Dig holes for the crowns about the same depth as the nursery pots they were in when you bought them. The crown should be around 2 inches below the soil line. Spread out the roots and firm the soil carefully around them. Water well and keep the soil around it consistently moist until you see new growth coming.

Strawberries bear fruit the first year you plant them, but as their root system adapts to your garden and they begin to spread, the yield increases. You can expect to harvest $\frac{1}{2}$ to 1 pound of strawberries from each plant in a season. You need 15 pounds of strawberries to make 5 gallons of wine.

Strawberry plants have a unique growing pattern. Other types of berries come up in the same spot each year because their roots survive from one year to the next. The tops, or canes, die after they produce fruit and the roots shoot up new ones each season. But after strawberries bear their fruit, the plants grow two- to three-foot-long roots, or runners, near the surface of the soil from which new plants grow. The "mother" plants may not survive cold winters, but the "daughters" are ready to fruit the following spring. If you don't interfere, your strawberry patch will fill into a dense mat of plants and runners within a few years, and will be loaded with fruit. To give them room to spread and reproduce like this, plant them so there's one crown per square foot.

CARE

For the first month after planting berries, they need consistent moisture. That doesn't mean you have to water them every day; just don't let them dry out. Once established, berry plants need to be watered only during extended dry spells. Likewise, compost added to the soil before planting gives them the nutrients they need to get established. An annual booster of a couple-inch layer of compost scratched into the surface of the soil is about all the fertilizing that berry plants need to stay healthy and productive.

Weeds are an enemy of berries because they suck moisture and nutrients away from the plants and harbor a few pests that threaten your berry crops. The first and always most reliable way to keep soil moist and weeds at bay is with mulch. Keep the soil around your berry plants covered with a 2- to 3-inch layer of natural materials such as grass clippings, leaves, or straw.

Strawberries are so named because our forebears grew them on beds covered in straw, a practice that kept the very vulnerable fruit off the soil and away from pests and diseases. If you can get straw from a local source, make sure you don't get hay instead—straw is just stems from cut grasses, whereas hay has seed heads, too, which will grow into next year's weeds.

Insects are not much of a problem for small berry plots, but larger pests can get to your berry crop before you. Birds plunder blueberry, gooseberry, and currant bushes, and seem to taste every strawberry in a plot. Rabbits and squirrels come for strawberries, too, and in many areas so do deer. Fences, scarecrows, flapping streamers, and whirligigs can help, but netting is your best chance of protecting your crop from wildlife. Spread it over the plants after the fruit forms but before it grows to its full size. And plan to share at least a little with your local critters.

Both yellow jacket hornets (they're not bees!) and Japanese beetles do occasionally plague suburban raspberry patches, but I've found that small, two-legged creatures with opposable thumbs—that is, my children and others in the neighborhood—are the most common cause of fruit loss. The best protection from this sort of loss that I can recommend is to not repeat my mistake of showing the kids how delicious the berries are right off the vine.

Raspberries and blackberries produce best if you take time each year to remove canes that have finished fruiting. Anytime after you've harvested the fruit, cut the canes that bore the berries to the ground, just above the crown. Blueberries grow on a different sort of shrub and do not need annual pruning, but they live longer (up to twenty years) and produce more when, every other year or so, you cut out canes that have become more than an inch in diameter, as well as any that are diseased or broken.

Strawberries renew themselves through their process of making daughter plants. After four to five seasons, though, the original plants begin to lose their vigor and productivity. Remove and replace them with new plants to keep your harvest coming.

HARVEST

Berries reach their peak of ripeness only on the vine. That is, they stop making sugar as soon as they are picked. They are also at their most fragile at that point. This explains why supermarket strawberries tend to be bland—they are picked before they are fully ripe and are still very firm so they can withstand shipping across the country. The good news for you is that you can wait until your berries have fully ripened on the bush, and you want to wait until the fruit has its full sweetness so that the wine you make with them has its full complement of flavors. There are a few challenges, though, that waiting presents. At peak ripeness, the berries are at their most appealing to birds and other pests, so you need to be extra vigilant about protecting them as they ripen. And when they pass peak ripeness, berries may become less sweet and more "winey," which is not desirable even if you want to make them into wine because it indicates the sugars have begun to naturally ferment, leaving less for the winemaking yeast to consume and turn into alcohol. Berries also become vulnerable to mold and other causes of rot as they age.

The key, then, is to pick your berries at their peak of ripeness. Color is an early sign that the berries are getting near that point, but after they turn their final color they still need a week or two after that to complete their ripening. Taste a couple each day after they've colored up to see how sweet they are becoming. When the taste hasn't changed for a few days, they're ready to be picked.

Ripe raspberries, blackberries, and blueberries almost drop into your hand or basket when you tickle them with your fingertips. If you need to pull them, they're not quite ripe. Gooseberries and currants come off the vine with the gentlest of tugs. You want to get strawberries with their green caps intact, so snip or pinch them from the stems rather than pulling on the berries.

If you are lucky enough to live where blackberries grow wild, you'll find them at their ripest in June (in the South) or July (North). Be aware when you go to pick wild berries that they are a favorite food of bears. Wineberries are native plants that look a lot like their close relative, raspberries—you'll see them growing wild along the untamed edges of suburban neighborhoods and other developed areas. They are safe to pick, eat, and make into wine, and as the name suggests, their taste is sourer than raspberries. In my research for this book, I found no one making wineberry wine, but you could substitute them for raspberries.

Try to begin your winemaking process as soon as you pick the berries. If you must wait a day or so, don't rinse any dirt off the berries until you are ready to prepare your must. Leftover moisture is an invitation to mold and other fungi.

MAKING WINE

If you grew up in the 1970s, like I did, you probably remember Boone's Farm Strawberry Hill wine. It came in a bottle with a screw top and was almost too sweet to drink—more like strawberry soda pop than wine. Of course, we didn't drink it because we liked the flavor—it was a cheap and easy way to get a little buzz. But berry wine need not taste like a soft drink or be just for getting sloshed. When fermented, each berry's natural tartness and acidity help to keep the sweetness from being overbearing. Berry wines have a bright, fruity flavor that give you a sense of warm summer days as you drink them.

AMOUNT OF FRUIT (FOR 5 GALLONS OF WINE):
  Blackberries: 10 pounds
  Blueberries: 15 pounds
  Currants: 20 pounds
  Gooseberries: 20 pounds
  Raspberries: 20 pounds
  Strawberries: 15 pounds

ADDITIONAL INGREDIENTS:
  Sugar: 10 to 11 pounds
  For strawberries: sliced lemons (two to three per 5 gallons of must),
    or 5 teaspoons acid blend
  Strong black tea (about $1/2$ cup per gallon), or 1 teaspoon wine tannins
  Yeast nutrient: 2 tablespoons
  Pectic enzyme: $3/4$ teaspoon

PREPARATION: Berries are loaded with tiny seeds and they pose the main challenge to turning your fruit into must. To keep them from leaving behind a bitter flavor and lots of debris, put the berries into a fine-mesh nylon bag (available from winemaking suppliers) and squeeze it with your hands until the juice flows into your bucket. After adding enough water so that you have 5 gallons of fluid, leave the bag in the bucket for forty-eight hours, then toss the pulp into your compost pile. After removing the bag, mix in the sugar until it is dissolved. Add the lemons, tea, pectic enzyme, and yeast nutrient, then wait forty-eight hours.

BEST YEAST: Montrachet Red

TIME TO FIRST RACK: Five days after pitching the yeast

TIME TO DRINK: One year or more

✕✕✕✕✕✕✕✕✕✕✕ ORCHARD FRUITS ✕✕✕✕✕✕✕✕✕✕✕

Wines you make from orchard fruits range from mildly flavored, such as those from apricots and peaches, to the intensely sweet drinks made of plums, cherries, or figs. You could compare the flavor of peach and apricot wines with eating a piece of fresh-baked pie while you sip on a glass of Chablis. Plums and cherries have darker, more nuanced flavors, and the wine you make from them is a rich raw material for distilling (see page 156). Figs are nearly as sweet as raisins, and they yield a sweet wine with a kind of nutty taste.

Growing these fruits yourself takes more time than berries, though contrary to what you might think, not necessarily a lot more space (I'll explain that later in this section). The investment that you put into waiting for fruit trees to reach a productive age is paid off as the years and even decades go by as they continue to bear fruit.

Just so you know, I know that apples and pears are orchard fruits, but they are better made into cider than wine, so I cover them in Chapter 4.

VARIETALS

APRICOTS are the earliest orchard fruits to bloom, so they can be vulnerable to losing flowers (which later turn into fruit) when hard frosts come in April and May. If you live where cold weather persists into spring, choose a late-blooming variety of apricot, such as Chinese (developed in Michigan) or Harlayne (from Ontario). If your climate is milder, you can plant earlier-blooming varieties, such as classic Moorpark or Goldcot. Standard-size apricot trees reach about 25 feet tall and 20 feet wide. You can find most varieties available as a semidwarf (15 to 20 feet tall) and as a dwarf (less than 15 feet), but bear in mind that smaller trees produce less fruit than standard-size trees.

CHERRIES can either be quite tart, such as those used to make pies or preserves, or very sweet, such as the dark red fruit you eat fresh in the summer. Either can be used to make wine, and in many cases they are blended together for a nicely balanced flavor. Sour cherries—often referred to as pie cherries—grow on trees that reach about 30 feet tall, a bit smaller than the standard size for sweet cherry trees, and they are the more cold-hardy of the two types. Sour cherries are self-pollinating, meaning that the trees bear fruit even when you plant only one of them. Montmorency has been the standard variety since the eighteenth century, and it is very cold tolerant and productive. The trees often live fifty years or longer, and for that reason can become very wide and tall. North Star and Meteor are widely adapted, produce lots of juicy fruit, and are available as semidwarf and dwarf trees for smaller spaces. Bing is the most familiar sweet cherry, but it is well suited only to mild climates and is vulnerable to diseases. Stella is more cold tolerant and disease resistant, and it begins bearing fruit at a comparatively young age. It also is self-fertile, so you can plant it alone, or include it when you plant other varieties because it works well as a pollinator. Starkcrimson is another self-fertile variety that naturally matures at less than 20 feet tall.

FIGS have been cultivated in the countries around the Mediterranean for thousands of years and are well-adapted to the conditions you find there—moderate temperatures and brilliantly sunny days. Mission, Brown Turkey, Kodata, and many traditional Italian varieties are productive in such climates as California and the Gulf Coast, but may not fare as well where summer weather doesn't last as long or where winters are colder. Celeste is more cold-tolerant and bears heavy loads of very sweet fruit. Hardy Chicago can take the cold but is not quite as productive. In climates warm enough for fig trees to grow year-round, they reach up to 30 feet tall, but they tend to peak at around 15 feet tall in regions where they need to be protected or dug up over the winter.

Unlike other fruit trees, figs can be grown by taking a cutting from an existing tree—you just clip off a shoot near the bottom of the trunk and put the cutting in a pot with a light soil and peat mix, keep it moist, and transplant it outside when it has grown at least four new leaves. If a neighbor or local farmer is growing figs, the variety is adapted to your climate and you can feel confident taking a cutting and planting it in your yard.

PEACHES must have a minimum of chilling hours (when temperatures stay at or below freezing) to continue growing and bearing fruit each season. The amount of chilling hours depends on the variety, and it is the first characteristic to consider when choosing a peach to grow. The farther south you live, the more important it is to choose a variety with low chilling requirements. You also can choose between clingstone (with flesh that sticks to the pit inside) or freestone (whose pit is not attached to the flesh) types, and varieties with either yellow or white flesh. Clingstones ripen early in the season (late June to early July in most regions) and tend to be smaller than freestones, but they also have the "peachiest" taste and a softer texture. Freestones are most popular for eating fresh—they're less messy, I suppose—but clingstones are the choice for pies, cobblers, preserves, and wine.

White-fleshed varieties are sweeter, juicier, and typically more fragile than the yellow types, but the yellows have the stronger, peachy flavor. Redhaven is a widely adapted yellow clingstone type that hits its peak of ripeness in early July. Sugar Giant is a white freestone that's exceptionally sweet (hence the name) and ready in mid to late July. For a later crop, Blake is a popular yellow freestone that is well adapted to a wide range of conditions. Peach trees typically top out at about 15 feet tall. You can find dwarf varieties that grow just 8 to 10 feet tall.

PLUMS have a natural astringency along with intense sweetness that suits them well to making wine. Plum wine is a traditional drink in Japan and China. In supermarkets here, you see mostly a few Japanese varieties of plums suited to commercial production, but you have lots of other choices when you grow your own or forage for the many wild types that grow in nearly every climate. The European (sometimes called Italian) types, the kind that are dried into prunes, are best adapted to growing in small yards and producing fruit for winemaking. Stanley is a proven performer that ripens its fruit near the end of August. It is also self-fertile, so you can plant just one tree, and it serves as a pollinator for many other varieties. Like most plum trees, it can grow up to 35 feet tall (and even higher), but a dwarf version won't grow beyond 15 feet.

Slightly less domesticated damsons and greengages are close relatives of plums with even more pronounced astringent flavors. You can find them in farmers' markets, to sample before you plant. The hardy beach plum, or shore plum, grows untended along the eastern shore from Maine to Delaware, so you could forage for the fruit or buy plants from nurseries in the region. The small shrubs are very hardy and fare well in dry, sandy soil.

SITE

Fruit trees need lots of sun to bear a healthy, substantial crop, but almost as important is air circulation. The diseases that can spoil tree fruit are mostly fungal, so you want as much air as possible passing in and around it, drying off the dampness that hosts mold and the like. Avoid spots where buildings, fences, and other large trees can block airflow. You'd be right if you are also guessing that drainage is critical for fruit trees for the same reasons that airflow matters.

The ideal location for growing fruit trees is on an east-facing slope so they get morning sun (helps to dry off dew) while water and frosty air in early spring flow down the slope and away from the trees.

Remember that trees get a lot bigger than they are when you plant them. Be sure your site has room for them to reach their full size and enough width so there's space between each tree. If you live where sunny space is limited, you can grow fruit trees in large containers. Container trees won't bear as much fruit or live as long as will those planted in the ground, but you can get a sufficient harvest from them to make a batch of wine. Be sure you have a plan for protecting them in winter, because they are more vulnerable to hard freezes. You can bring them in to an unheated garage or wrap them in burlap to help them survive the frigid months.

SOIL

Fruit trees need soil that drains well, but they are otherwise tolerant of a wide range of conditions. Choosing a site where water doesn't puddle is the most valuable step you can take to ensure sufficient drainage. Breaking up compacted soil when you dig the planting holes improves drainage and helps young saplings' roots grow sturdy and strong early and establish themselves quickly. Work compost into the soil before you plant, too, so that it has a healthy supply of beneficial microbes to help those roots access the nutrients in the soil.

For the first few seasons after planting, spread an inch or two of compost on the soil around the tree's dripline (the perimeter within which raindrops drip from the branches) in spring and fall. In between, keep a constant layer of organic mulch (grass clippings, shredded leaves, or straw), which gradually nourish the roots as they break down.

Apricots are the most adaptable tree fruit to the alkaline soils that are common in the Southwest and other regions. Cherries, figs, peaches, and plums fare well wherever the soil pH is not extremely low (below 5.8) or high (above 8.0).

PLANTING

Apricot, cherry, peach, and plum trees begin producing a substantial amount of fruit three to four years after you plant them and they reach their peak of production within five years after that. Fig trees mature a bit earlier than these other fruits—you will be picking your first figs in two to three years. Each of these types of fruit trees can produce about 20 pounds of fruit or more each season, more than enough for a batch of wine.

Except in the northernmost states and Canada, early fall is the best time to plant fruit trees. Early spring (after the average last frost date) is the ideal planting time in colder climates and is the next best season to plant everywhere else. Soak the trees' roots in a bucket of room-temperature water overnight or at least a couple of hours before planting.

If the soil is very dry, moisten (but don't soak) it before you start digging. This helps to loosen the soil and makes it easier to dig. Carve out a hole that's a few inches deeper than the tree's root-ball and up to 6 inches larger in diameter. Loosen the soil as much as you can in the bottom and around the sides of the hole. In the bottom of the hole, make a small mound of soil and then set the tree on top of it, gently spreading the roots out over the mound.

Nearly all apricot, cherry, peach, and plum trees are grafted, meaning that roots adapted to your conditions are melded to a trunk that produces the variety of fruit that you want. You can see the graft union near the base of the tree's trunk. To protect that union and ensure you get the fruit you're expecting, place the tree high in your planting hole so that its graft union is a few inches above ground level.

Backfill the hole with soil and compost until it is just about level with the ground around it. You don't want to mound soil up around the trunk; rather, create a kind of very shallow dish around the tree so that water runs down to the roots instead of shedding away from the tree. Gently pat the soil around the base of the tree to firm it into place, taking care not to pack it down too tightly and suffocate the roots.

Where deer and other four-legged pests gnaw on the tender bark and shoots of new trees, protect yours by wrapping them loosely in chicken wire or white plastic tubes that you can get at nurseries. Staking young trees is vital in very windy areas, and it can be helpful in most places. If you do stake, be sure you leave enough leeway for the tree to sway and bend in the wind, so that the roots develop a strong grip on the soil and yet remain pliable. Use a small piece of garden hose or other rubber protection to keep rope from digging into the young trees' bark. Leave stakes in place for no more than five years.

CARE

Young fruit trees need a consistent supply of moisture while they're getting established. Water them once a week when it hasn't rained. After three or four years, the trees' roots are deep enough that you don't need to water anymore, except in an extended drought. Likewise, a twice-a-year application of compost helps nourish trees when they're young, but as the trees mature they find the nutrients they need deep in the soil. Container trees, however, need to be watered during dry spells (even in winter) and fed with compost when they start leafing out each season, after they bloom, and after you've harvested the fruit. Beware of overwatering container trees, which can drown them. Push your index finger into the soil, and if you feel moisture of any kind, wait until the soil below the surface is dry before watering again.

Mulches such as grass clippings, leaves, and straw build soil as they break down, keep weeds away from the trees, and conserve moisture for the trees. Bark chips don't break down and feed the soil, but they do help in keeping weeds down and holding in moisture. Keep any of these mulches around your fruit trees throughout their lives, or if that's for some reason not possible, at least be sure to keep grass and other weeds from growing up tall around the trees.

Fruit trees tend to start more fruit than the tree can sustain. When the fruit is still small (late spring or early summer, depending on the variety), the trees typically shed a portion of it. The simplest yet most important way to keep fruit trees healthy and problem free is to clean up fallen fruit and leaves around them. Pests and diseases move into this debris, reproduce, and then work their up to the tree. You can compost the debris you pick up, but it is best to use the compost on other plants in your garden, because some of the problems may survive the heat in a compost heap.

Pruning is essential for keeping trees healthy, too. You can cut off any dead or diseased limbs whenever you see them. After the tree is more than five years old, lop off branches that crowd other limbs (keep the stronger-looking one), cross through the middle of the tree, or otherwise block air from flowing freely around the fruit. The best time for this annual pruning is in winter, when the tree is dormant.

Commercial fruit producers use a variety of chemical fungicides to protect their crop and even organic growers may use copper or sulfur sprays for the same purpose. If you've ensured that your trees have good air circulation and drainage, and you've cleaned up the area around them consistently, your fruit will be less prone to problems with fungus. And because you are planning to use the fruit to make wine, it need not be as cosmetically perfect as supermarket produce. Should you find that the fungal invasion goes beyond your tolerance level, try using a spray made with 3 tablespoons of baking soda and a squirt of dish soap in a quart of water. It's a nontoxic treatment that controls a variety of fungi and leaves behind no residues that affect the flavor of your wine.

Birds can be devastating pests of cherries. If you plant a dwarf-size tree, you may be able to cover it with nylon netting like that used for covering berry bushes. For taller trees, you can try tying reflective tape or (my grandparents' favorite) putting aluminum foil pie plates as high in the tree as you can get. I won't promise this will protect your entire crop from birds, but it just might preserve enough cherries for you to make a batch or two of wine.

Where winters are short and not too harsh, fig trees can grow outside all year long. In regions with colder climates, fig growers protect the trees by digging them up and either bringing them inside wrapped in a breathable cloth, such as burlap (where winters are truly frigid), or burying them outside beneath a sheltering blanket of loose soil, fall leaves, or other natural mulch. The trees are replanted after the last frost in spring and continue their annual growth. You can ensure you'll always have fresh fig trees if you take a cutting each year and start it as described on page 62).

HARVEST

Tree fruits reach their peak of flavor and sweetness only while still on the branches. They often turn to their final color a few weeks before they are at their ripest, so you'll want to wait patiently for them to finish. A gentle tug should be enough force to pull a ripe fruit from the tree; if you need to pull harder, the fruit is not yet ripe. As with other fruits, tasting the fruit as it ripens helps you determine when they've stopped becoming sweeter and juicier.

Try to pick your fruit no more than a day or so before you plan to make your wine. If a heavy storm is forecast, you want to pick all the fruit before it's blown to the ground. Store it, if you must, in a cool, dark place with low humidity. Your refrigerator is not ideal because such cool temperatures can stop the ripening process and begin to turn some of the fruit's sugars to less-flavorful starches.

At their full ripeness, these fruits can become quite soft and easily bruised. Use shallow boxes and small buckets when harvesting them to keep the ones on top from smashing those at the bottom. Cut off any bruised parts before you start making wine—you don't want spoiled flavors to carry over into your must.

MAKING WINE

AMOUNT OF FRUIT (FOR 5 GALLONS OF WINE):
Apricots, peaches, or figs: 15 pounds
Cherries or plums: 20 pounds

ADDITIONAL INGREDIENTS:
Sugar: 9 to 10 pounds
Sliced lemons (two to three per 5 gallons of must), or 2 tablespoons acid blend
Black tea (about $1/2$ cup per gallon), or $1/2$ to 1 teaspoon wine tannins
Pectic enzyme: $1/2$ to 1 teaspoon
Yeast nutrient: 2 tablespoons

PREPARATION: Boil a gallon of water. Remove the pits from your stone fruits.
If you don't want to pit the cherries, put them in a nylon bag and crush them with your hands over the bucket, and put the bag in the bucket. Chop apricots, peaches, plums, or figs into wedges. When the water has boiled, pour it into your primary fermentation bucket, squeeze the fruit, and drop it into the bucket.

With the water and fruit in the bucket, add the sugar. Cover and wait twenty-four hours. Add the lemons, tea, pectic enzyme, and yeast nutrient, cover, and wait another twenty-four hours to pitch the yeast. Remove the bag of cherry pits and skins before pitching the yeast, or strain out the other fruit's pulp and skins when you rack for the first time.

BEST YEAST: Montrachet Red for cherries or plums, EC-1118 for apricots or peaches, K1V-116 for figs
TIME TO FIRST RACK: Five days
TIME TO DRINK: One year

✕✕✕✕✕✕✕✕✕✕✕✕ CITRUS FRUITS ✕✕✕✕✕✕✕✕✕✕✕✕✕

Oranges, grapefruits, tangerines, lemons, and limes bring all the key flavor components—sweetness, acidity, and bitterness—to winemaking. They become light, refreshing wines that treat you to a taste of the tropics. Citrus wines pair well with seafood and spicy dishes, and they're ideal for making spritzers you'll enjoy while watching the sun set on a large body of water, or at least imagining that you are.

Citrus trees, as you probably know, are subtropical plants, and cannot survive freezing temperatures. If you live in Florida or California, or along the Gulf Coast, you can grow citrus trees in your yard year-round. Many types of citrus trees also grow well in containers, so you can harvest your own fruit in even the coldest climates. I have information for you here on how to do both.

VARIETALS

Citrus trees reach 25 to 30 feet tall at full maturity, which is about five years after planting them. They are nearly all self-fertile, meaning you don't have to plant a second tree to ensure the flowers are pollinated and form fruit.

GRAPEFRUIT has a complicated genealogy (it may or may not be a cross between oranges and pomelo, a similar wild subtropical fruit), but for your purposes you need only to know that you can choose yellow- or red-fleshed varieties. Duncan is a classic white with lots of juice as well as seeds. Marsh is a newer, less seedy white. Star Ruby has the reddest flesh, pink juice, and no seeds, and the fruit tends to be small. Where temperatures are closer to tropical, you can grow Rio Red, an extra-sweet seedless red. The two red varieties are available as dwarf trees. Oroblanco (a.k.a. Sweetie) is a yellow seedless variety that adapts well to containers.

LEMONS AND LIMES are the easiest citrus to grow in the ground or in containers. You may have tasted, or at least heard about, Meyer lemons (no relation to me) and Kaffir limes. Both have distinctive flavors and they are very productive, even in pots. I once worked in an office with a Meyer lemon in a pot that was watered mostly by the dregs of coffee cups and that never got closer to real sun than the skylight 25 feet above, yet it reliably produced a nice crop of fruit every year. If you want to make interesting blush wines, go with Sungold or Variegated Pink lemons.

ORANGES AND TANGERINES are closely related though they are not the same species. They are both sweeter than the other citrus fruits, and the juice holds its pale orange color through fermentation. Trovita orange is a juicing (rather than a navel) type available as a dwarf that performs well in climates where summers are not scorching. Blood oranges, which have dark flesh and juice for which they are named, do need very hot days and cool nights (as you find in their native Mediterranean climate) to produce well. Sour oranges are a good choice for growing in containers in cooler climates and for making tart wine. Tangerines are sometimes called mandarins, though they may be a different but very similar species. Gold Nugget is very tolerant of a wide range of conditions and bears loads of small but very sweet seedless tangerines in the ground or a container.

SITE

Citrus trees need long days of direct sunlight to ripen their fruit. Avoid planting them where they will be shaded by buildings or other trees.

Growing the trees in containers allows you to move them to get the maximum amount of sun as the light's angle gradually changes during the growing season. When you bring your potted trees in for the winter, put them near a west- or south-facing window to get them the most light possible during the season.

SOIL

Sandy, slightly acidic soil is commonplace where citrus tends to grow, but it can tolerate denser soil and a more neutral pH. Drainage is vitally important, so if your soil has a moderate to heavy clay content, work compost and sphagnum peat moss into the planting hole before setting your trees in.

For containers, your ideal soil mix is not bagged potting soil and most definitely not the ordinary soil you dig up in your yard (it's much too heavy for growing anything in containers). Instead, go with a mix of 50 percent well-aged compost (homemade or bought in a bag at a nursery or home center) and 50 percent peat moss, thoroughly blended together.

PLANTING

A standard-size citrus tree can produce as much as 90 pounds of fruit in a season. Trees growing in containers are more likely to produce (depending on the variety and conditions) 25 to 30 pounds of fruit in a season.

Soak the roots of your citrus trees in a bucket of tepid water for up to twenty-four hours before you are ready to plant. Prepare an outdoor site in late March to early April by digging holes few inches wider than the trees' root-balls and the same depth as the roots are in the nursery container. Make a small mound in the center of the hole. Set the tree's roots on top of the soil mound you made, but make sure the graft union stays above the soil line after you've backfilled the hole. (For an explanation of the graft union, see page 65.)

Water the tree well after planting. If you live where winds can be strong, stake the tree for the first three years, taking care not to tie it too tightly—you don't want the rope to damage the trunk and you want the tree to sway a bit, so that it develops sturdy roots and a stout trunk.

For growing in a pot, choose a container that's at least 20-gallon size, and a 30- or even 40-gallon one would be even better as the tree matures. Just as if you were planting in the ground, set the tree in the container so that the graft union is above the soil line. Gently water the soil mix as you add it to the container so that it washes down and surrounds the roots and closes up any air pockets in the soil.

CARE

Newly planted trees (in the ground) need consistent moisture for the first year after you put them in. After that, they should have roots deep enough to pull moisture from the soil except during very dry spells. Citrus trees, especially those growing in sandy soil, benefit from regular applications of fertilizer. Espoma Citrus-tone and Dr. Earth's Organic 9 Fruit Tree Fertilizer are two reliable granulated organic plant foods. Start fertilizing your tree after you see new growth the first year and then repeat in early spring and after the harvest each year.

A yearly pruning helps to keep your citrus tree vibrant and productive. Late winter, before the tree blooms, is the best time to prune it. Start but cutting off any suckers, or shoots that come up from the roots or below the graft union. Clip them off right at the trunk or root. Then cut out branches and twigs that crowd or cross over other branches. You want to cut away any growth that impedes sunlight and air from reaching the center of the tree's canopy.

Container trees need even more consistent pruning than trees planted in the ground. On top, trim back branches in late winter (before they flower in spring) so that the tree stays below 5 feet tall. About every five years, lift the tree out of its container and cut off roots that are wrapping around the outside of the root-ball and a few of the thickest and woodiest of all the roots. Repot it with a fresh mix of compost and peat.

HARVEST

In tropical regions, where temperatures are warm all year and the day length (the number of hours of light and dark) remains consistent, the skin of all citrus fruits stays green even when it's ripe. Only in more northern climates does the fruit change to yellow or orange. (The cause of the color change is the same as it is for leaves in the fall—with declining daylight hours, the plant produces less chlorophyll, which is the source of the green.)

Color change, then, is not an indicator of ripeness in citrus fruits. To further complicate the challenge of picking your citrus fruit at its sweetest and ripest, it hangs on the tree long after it is ripe and even begins to decay while still attached. Tasting the fruit is the only reliable way to tell when the fruit is ripest. Start trying it a few weeks after it reaches its full size. When the flavor hasn't changed for a week, the fruit is ready for picking. Be patient, though—citrus fruit does not ripen any more after it is picked.

MAKING WINE

AMOUNT OF FRUIT (FOR 5 GALLONS OF WINE): 25 to 30 pounds

ADDITIONAL INGREDIENTS:
Sugar: 10 pounds
Strong black tea (about $^1/_2$ cup per gallon), or 1 teaspoon wine tannins
Yeast nutrient: 2 tablespoons

PREPARATION: Citrus juice is rich in sugars and acid, and the skin and pith have a slightly bitter taste, and you want to get all of those flavors into your must. Start by slicing the fruit into halves or quarters and squeeze out as much of the juice as possible into your primary fermentation bucket. Retrieve and discard any seeds you find. Add the rinds to the juice and pour in a gallon of boiling water. Wait for twenty-four hours, then add another gallon of boiling water and the sugar, tea, and yeast nutrient. Wait another twenty-four hours, then spoon or strain out the rinds, and pitch the yeast. Strain out the pulp on the first racking.

BEST YEAST: Champagne
TIME TO FIRST RACK: Four to five days
TIME TO DRINK: Eighteen months

✕✕✕✕✕✕✕✕✕✕✕✕✕ ROOT CROPS ✕✕✕✕✕✕✕✕✕✕✕✕✕

Parsnips—long, white roots that look a lot like carrots—are high in sugar and have a long history as a winemaking ingredient in the British Isles. Authors such as Thomas Hardy, among others, make reference to parsnip wine in novels; and John Seymour, the guru of modern homesteading, reportedly preferred it over any other kind of homemade wine. A couple of generations back, parsnips were a common vegetable in the American diet, but they don't show up on a lot of dinner tables and restaurant menus these days. Wines made from root vegetables, including carrots and beets as well as parsnips, are naturally sweet because these ingredients are very high in sugar. Their earthier flavors balance sugars, yielding a wine that is quite sweet but with woody undertones.

VARIETALS

PARSNIP varieties are limited, most likely because so few gardeners or commercial growers are planting them. Hollow Crown produces 12-inch-long tapered roots about 105 days after planting. Cobham Improved Marrow makes shorter roots (less than 10 inches) that are especially sweet. Harris Model takes a little longer to mature—up to 120 days—and its 10- to 12-inch-long roots are very white and smooth.

CARROTS, on the other hand, offer you many choices. And when you choose, you'll see such cultivars as Imperator, Nantes, Danvers, and Chantenay. Imperators are the long, tapered, evenly shaped carrots you mostly see in the supermarket. They tend to be the least flavorful kinds of carrots and not the easiest to grow unless you have sandy soil. Nantes are the carrot to grow for winemaking because they have the most sugar and the least starch of the different types. The roots are shorter and thicker than the Imperators'. If your soil is dense clay, the Chantenays make shorter, wider roots, which works best when they can't grow too deep belowground.

BEETS are one of the best garden crops to grow because they give you two harvests—the aboveground leaves that are tasty in a salad or sautéed, and the roots that grow belowground. Many heirloom and unusual varieties of beets are available today, including golden and striped. For a wine with a dark red color and a hefty supply of sweetness, Detroit Dark Red is a very reliable performer in a wide range of conditions.

SITE

Root crops grow best in full sun, but can produce in partial shade. Parsnips and carrots need a long season to mature, so you want to plant them where they won't be disturbed or in the way of other crops you want to grow. Beets take just fifty to seventy days to produce their crop, so you can put them in a spot in your garden where you want to plant other crops during the season.

SOIL

The looser your soil, the bigger and better your root crops will be. If your soil is on the sandy side, you're already well on your way. But if your soil is heavier, you can dig in the spot where you want to plant the roots down to 12 inches or more deep. Blend the soil with an equal amount of compost as you shovel it back into the trench you've dug. Adding sand to clay soil doesn't work to loosen it because it causes the clay soil to clump. If you can't dig down deep enough, build a raised bed by mounding up a blend of soil and compost 6 to 8 inches above the ground level. Framing the raised bed with wood (not pressure-treated wood, which is toxic) or bricks helps to keep the soil from eroding away.

PLANTING

Beets, carrots, and parsnips are easy to grow from seeds you plant right in the garden. From an 8-foot row, you can expect to harvest about 8 pounds of beets or parsnips, and about ten to twelve pounds of carrots.

In early spring, after nighttime temperatures stay above freezing most of the time, soak the seeds for a few hours the day you are ready to plant them. Carve out a 1/2-inch-deep furrow in the soil and plant the seeds about $1/2$ inch to an inch apart. Parsnip seeds tend to have a low germination rate, so you can sow them a little more thickly. Beets and carrots are fairly reliable germinators, and don't need to be planted as thickly.

Cover the seeds with a layer of soil and pat it gently to be sure the seeds have contact with the soil, but don't tamp it down so the seeds can't break through. Water gently and cover the soil with a very light and loose layer of straw (not hay) or dried grass clippings. Be sure the soil where you planted the seeds stays consistently moist until you see three or more leaves aboveground. Be patient: These types of seeds can take two to three weeks before they sprout up.

CARE

Once your root crops are up and producing healthy green growth on top, add more straw or grass mulch to the bed to keep the soil from crusting over and prevent weeds from moving in. Also, switch from daily light watering to deep soaking once or twice a week to encourage the roots to grow deeper into the soil.

To reach their full size, your root crops need elbow room. Unless you were very careful about spacing when planting your seeds, the little seedlings will be too close together. You need to thin them out. This is a challenge, I know—you have to kill some of the tiny little sprouts that you've grown and that's hard to do. But suck it up and do it for the good of those left behind. Look at the sprouts every 2 to 4 inches in the row and select the biggest and the sturdiest. Gently pull out the others. In the case of beets, you can eat the thinnings, but with carrots and parsnips you can just compost them.

Root crops depend on a variety of nutrients, including minerals, in the soil. But you have to provide those—ideally in the form of compost—before you plant. Once your seedlings have come up, they do not need to be fertilized. Keep a constant two- to three-inch layer of straw or dried grass mulch on the bed where your roots are growing, which will nourish the soil as it decomposes and hold moisture in the soil.

As the roots grow larger, they may begin to push their tops out of the top of the soil. Protect them from exposure to the sun, which can change their color and flavor, by mounding up soil over them so that only the leafy green tops are visible.

HARVEST

Beets are ready to harvest sixty to seventy days after you plant the seeds. Be sure not to wait much longer than that to harvest them, because as they get older they become woodier and less sweet. Parsnips and carrots take just about the full gardening season to mature. And when they remain in the ground through a light frost or two, they convert more of their starches to sugar, making them sweeter and even better for making wine.

Take care when harvesting your root crops not to damage them as they come out of the ground. Work carefully with a spade or garden fork to lift them out. If the ground is dry and hard, moisten it before you try to dig up the roots.

MAKING WINE

AMOUNT OF VEGETABLE (FOR 5 GALLONS OF WINE): 12 to 14 pounds

ADDITIONAL INGREDIENTS:
Sugar: 9 pounds
Sliced lemons (two to three in 5 gallons of must), or 1 teaspoon acid blend
Strong black tea (about 1/2 cup per gallon of must), or 2 teaspoons wine tannins
Yeast nutrient: 2 tablespoons
Yeast energizer: 1 tablespoon

PREPARATION: Scrub the vegetables thoroughly and remove the tops. Cut the roots into large chunks, then add them to 2 gallons of boiling water and simmer until they are tender but not falling apart. Remove from heat, skim out the vegetables (and eat or compost them), and add the sugar, stirring to dissolve thoroughly. Add other ingredients, then let sit covered for twenty-four hours. If you've used lemons, skim them out before pitching the yeast.

BEST YEAST: Epernay
TIME TO FIRST RACK: Five days
TIME TO DRINK: Eighteen months

╳╳╳╳╳╳╳╳╳╳╳ SUMMER VEGETABLES ╳╳╳╳╳╳╳╳╳╳╳

You can use many garden vegetables to make wine, particularly tomatoes, chile peppers, cucumbers, and watermelons. Their flavors, which range from the acidity of tomatoes to the spiciness of the peppers to the sweetness of watermelons, will be preserved in the wine, giving you a fresh taste of summer whenever you drink them. They are among the easiest wine ingredients to grow, especially if you don't have the space needed to grow tree fruits or even berries.

VARIETALS

CUCUMBERS may either be salad varieties, with smooth skin, a lot of seeds, and a very mild flavor; or picklers, with bumpy thicker skin, few seeds, and a hint of bitterness. Either works for winemaking, but the pickling types are more productive and less prone to problems, they have fewer seeds for you to deal with, and the bitterness adds depth to your wine's flavor. County Fair is a very productive, disease-resistant pickler that is nearly seedless. If you prefer to grow the salad type (also called slicing cucumbers), Sweet Success is a thin-skinned, sweet, and disease-resistant choice. Whichever type you choose, consider that vining types can be grown up a trellis, so they take up less space in your garden than the bush types do.

CHILE PEPPERS range from mildly hot jalapeños to blistering habaneros and Ghost peppers. Beneath the spicy taste are more subtle flavors of sweetness and fruitiness that fermentation helps to highlight. Poblanos are slightly more spicy than jalapeños, and they are little larger, too. New Mexico is also on the mild end of the heat range—though hotter than poblanos—and they are exceptionally productive. Drinking wine made from the hottest peppers may not appeal to you, but you might like it as a marinade.

TOMATOES have long been the most popular crop for home gardeners—probably because you can't buy a good one in the supermarket—and they offer you almost countless variety choices. Cherry tomatoes are easiest to grow and most productive, and they are exceptionally sweet. They do tend to be low in acidity, as do yellow varieties, and they lack the deeper flavors of the larger, slower-growing beefsteak types. Heirloom varieties are enjoying a revival of interest and, while they are not the most productive, they regularly win taste comparisons. Two beefsteak heirlooms make excellent wine ingredients. Brandywine is the most widely available heirloom tomato. Cherokee Purple is both beautiful—with its deep red colors—and it tastes of plums and melon. If you want a more productive and disease-resistant large tomato, go with Park's Whopper. You can also now find varieties that stay green even when ripe. They tend to be more tart, a flavor that adds depth to your wine.

WATERMELONS need space for the vines to spread out and a long, hot summer to ripen. If you can give them those conditions, you can harvest enough big and juicy fruit for a batch of wine and to enjoy eating fresh. You might be tempted to plant one of the new seedless varieties now available, but that may make winemaking harder, not easier. That's because seedless varieties aren't truly seedless—they have soft white seeds you can swallow, as opposed to the hard, black ones you spit out. The soft white seeds are bound to get in your must and you'll have to strain them out later. The black seeds are easier to see and remove before you turn the juice into must. Crimson Sweet bears medium-size fruit with crisp flesh. Picnic watermelons are a little smaller and tolerant of a wide range of conditions. Moon and Stars is a cool heirloom with yellow markings on the dark green rind that look a bit like, well, moon and stars.

SITE

Full summer sun is essential for these garden crops to be as productive and hassle-free as possible. Unless you live in the Deep South, plant the crops where they can absorb the afternoon sunshine—that is, facing west. (They benefit from a little afternoon shade in scorching climates.) Like most crops, cucumbers, chile peppers, tomatoes, and watermelons need good drainage so they don't sit in water after heavy rains.

Watermelons grow on long vines that can quickly gobble up all the space in your garden. Look for a place to grow them where they can spread out 8 to 10 feet in all directions.

SOIL

A healthy supply of organic matter in the soil is the start to a productive garden. Homemade compost is the best way to add organic matter to your soil before and after planting. If you don't have compost, you can mix dried grass clippings and shredded fall leaves into the soil three to four weeks before planting.

Where digging is hard and improving the soil with organic matter a challenge, build raised beds by mounding a blend of soil and compost 8 to 12 inches above ground level. Raised beds drain well and are loose enough for plants' roots to spread out.

PLANTING

A productive cucumber plant bears 8 to 10 pounds of fruit. Beefsteak tomatoes can give you 15 or more pounds of fruit per plant, whereas plum tomatoes are more likely to be near 10 pounds. A chile pepper plant yields 5 to 8 pounds of fruit. You will be doing well if you pick three to five watermelons from each vine.

You can just purchase transplants at the local nursery to start your garden, but you get the widest choice when you grow cucumbers, peppers, tomatoes and watermelon from seeds. Unless you have a very long growing season, you need to start the seeds indoors under lights—no special grow lights needed; ordinary fluorescent "shop" lights work fine for this purpose—about six to eight weeks before the average last frost date in your area. (Your county's extension office, and every county has one, can tell you this date.) About two weeks before the last frost date, start taking the seedlings outside for a few hours and gradually increase the amount of time they are exposed to fresh air and direct sunlight. When the danger of frost has passed, plant them outside in your garden. Starting with transplants you buy is easier than growing from seeds. After the last frost, plant them or the seedlings you've raised in holes about the same depth as the container they were growing in. Exception: Put tomatoes in holes up to their lowest branches, because the stems will grow roots and produce a bigger, sturdier plant. The best time to plant in your garden is on an overcast day, so that the seedlings have time to acclimate to the soil before they get a full day of sunshine.

Water the seedlings before you plant them and keep the soil consistently moist until you see new green growth on them.

Watermelon growers often plant their seedlings in clusters of three or four on hills, or mounds of soil. This uses space efficiently, because you can plant closer than you would if you made rows, and still allows them room to spread out. As they grow, you will gently guide the long vines to grow away from the hill and the other vines on it.

CARE

When your seedlings have started growing again after you've transplanted them, which can take a few days, water them only once or twice a week. Direct the water to the soil, not the plants' leaves, and give them a good soaking so that the moisture reaches deep. This encourages the plants to grow deeper roots as they scavenge for water, and that will help the plants grow bigger and more productive, and find nutrients they need in the soil.

About two weeks after transplanting, begin feeding the seedlings with a dilute liquid organic fertilizer made with fish and seaweed. You can buy this in most nurseries and even home centers today under brand names such as Alaska and Neptune's Harvest. Repeat the feeding every two to three weeks until the plants' begin to flower, the beginning of their reproductive cycle.

Keep a constant layer of organic mulch, such as dried grass clippings, shredded leaves, or straw (not hay), on top of the soil throughout the growing season. Support for your cucumber, pepper, and tomato plants gets them off the ground and away from potential insect and disease problems lurking in the soil. For cucumbers, set up a trellis made from stakes and netting, and gently guide the vines onto the netting. You can use cages or stakes to hold up your tomatoes and peppers. For the big heirloom tomato plants, use the sturdiest of stakes or cages; as the fruit ripens it becomes heavy enough to topple flimsier supports.

HARVEST

Cucumbers are sweetest and juiciest when picked young. Pickling types are ready for harvest when they are 3 to 4 inches long. Slicing types are ripe when they are 6 to 8 inches long. Check cucumbers often; during the height of the season they can grow an inch or more each day.

Green peppers, whether hot or sweet, are not ripe. This can test your patience, but wait for your peppers to turn red, orange, or yellow before you pick them and you will enjoy the full range of their flavors. If you are anxious to try them, pick a few of the first green peppers, which will encourage the plant to set more that you can leave on the plant until they fully ripen.

Tomatoes gradually ripen as they turn from green to red. Wait to pick them after they change color, because they convert a lot of starch to sugar during the last two to three weeks of ripening. When the flesh yields a little from thumb pressure, they are ripe. After harvesting, do not put tomatoes in your refrigerator. Cold causes the fruit to change some of its sugars back to starch and makes the flesh mealy and less juicy.

Many people have developed their own tricks for recognizing when a watermelon is ripe and a couple of these methods are truly reliable. The first and most important indicator is to look at the end where the fruit is attached to the vine. The connection yellows and begins to turn brown as the fruit ripens. The part of the rind that sits on the ground also starts to yellow from a greenish white tint. Gently rap the melon with your fist. A ripe melon gives a dull thud; an unripe one still sounds a bit hollow. Like tomatoes, watermelons convert starch to sugar during their final days on the vine. This ends once the melons are picked. Wait until you are certain they're ripe before you harvest them.

MAKING WINE

AMOUNT OF FRUIT (FOR 5 GALLONS OF WINE):
Cucumbers: 20 pounds
Tomatoes: 20 pounds
Chile peppers: 10 pounds
Watermelons: 2 gallons of watermelon juice (3 to 5 large melons)

ADDITIONAL INGREDIENTS:
Sugar: 9 to 11 pounds (the least for watermelon, the most for peppers)
For cucumbers and watermelons: Sliced lemons (two or three per 5 gallons of must), or
  2 tablespoons acid blend
For chile peppers: 2 pounds raisins, chopped
Strong black tea ($^1/_2$ cup per gallon of must), or 1 to 2 teaspoons wine tannins
Pectic enzyme: $^1/_2$ teaspoon
Yeast nutrient: 2 tablespoons

PREPARATION: Cut cucumbers or tomatoes (cores removed) into chunks, then place the chunks in a nylon bag and into the primary fermentation bucket. Pour in a gallon of boiling water. Add the sliced lemons (if using), tea, and sugar. Stir until the sugar is dissolved, let cool, and add pectic enzyme and yeast nutrient. Wait twenty-four hours, then pitch the yeast. After primary fermentation—about five days later—remove the bag and lemons, squeezing as much juice as possible out of it into the must. Compost what's left in the bag. Pitch the yeast.

Roast chile peppers, freeze them for an hour or so, then remove their skins. Put them, along with chopped raisins and sliced lemons, in a bag. Boil a gallon of water, drop in the bag, and simmer for twenty minutes. After the water has cooled, pour it into the primary fermentation bucket and add the bag. Cover and let steep for twenty-four hours, then add 4 gallons of warm water. Stir in the sugar until it is dissolved and add the pectic enzyme and yeast nutrient. Pitch the yeast.

Slice watermelon and scoop out the flesh. Put it in a blender or food processor and pulse until the pulp has mostly liquefied. Pour it into the bucket and add the sliced lemons and 2 gallons of boiling water. Let it sit covered for twenty-four hours, then add another gallon of boiling water and the sugar. Stir until the sugar is dissolved. When cool, add the pectic enzyme and yeast nutrient. Twenty-four hours later, pitch the yeast.

BEST YEAST: Montrachet White or Lalvin E-1118
TIME TO FIRST RACK: Five to seven days
TIME TO DRINK: One year

✕✕✕✕ SPOTLIGHT ON: DOMAINE DE LA VALLÉE DU BRAS, ✕✕✕✕ BAIE ST-PAUL, QUEBEC

YOU'D EXPECT A VINTNER WITH THE APPELLATION "DOMAINE DE LA VALLÉE DU Bras" to turn out fine wines, but you wouldn't figure there'd be no grapes in its award-winning aperitif. In fact, you'd be surprised to find that the sweet, golden wine with an 18 percent ABV is made from carefully selected tomato varieties. Yes, tomatoes.

The wine has been created with a family recipe by Pascal Miche, whose great-grand-father developed it to capitalize on an exceptionally rich tomato harvest one summer in his native Belgium. The family has been making and sharing the wine for decades, but never sold it or released the recipe. Miche, now living on hilly slopes overlooking the Saint Lawrence River in Quebec, spent ten years testing tomato varieties and tinkering with the recipe before introducing his wine, Omerto (named for the recipe's creator, Omer) to the public in 2011.

A wine connoisseur and food industry consultant, Miche still isn't sharing his recipe, but he has acknowledged that among the varieties he uses are Sub Arctic, yellow, and black cherry tomatoes. These selections have the blend of acids and flavor components he wants for the wine, and they are highly productive in the short growing season in Quebec. He adds sugar to the fruit to get the alcohol content to reach 18 percent.

He offers two versions of Omerto: Moelleux (sweet) and Sec (dry). They are both sweeter than most grape wines, and the taste of tomatoes comes through mostly as a lightly tart flavor after you've swallowed. In his first year, Miche produced seventeen thousand bottles of the wine, and by his second, he had already sold thirty-four thousand. You can learn more about Miche and his wines, and plan a visit to his scenic tasting center, at domainevb.ca.

The first wines that people made (as opposed to those that were discovered after they had naturally fermented) were almost certainly made with foraged ingredients, such as wild grapes or berries. In the modern world, you might think foraging for food is only for survivalists and others who live far away from civilization, but even people living in cities and suburbs can find a lot of fresh and healthy ingredients for winemaking right in their neighborhoods, growing untended and waiting to be picked. If you look around, you can often find cherries, berries, crab apples, and other kinds of fruit that may have been planted decades ago and then forgotten. In many areas, urban foragers have even posted Google Maps highlighting spots where you can find such treasures.

Chokecherries, elderberries, and mulberries, honeysuckle, and the much-loathed lawn weed, dandelion, are all readily available ingredients that make for unique, delicious wines. Before we get into foraging, I need to remind you of two important warnings. First, be sure to accurately identify any plant before you eat it. Use a guidebook, or even better, go with an experienced forager. Second, eat plants you find only if you can be sure they have not been treated with lawn and garden chemicals.

GATHERING

CHOKECHERRIES were a staple food for the Native American tribes of the Plains—they were an essential ingredient in pemmican, the dried meat jerky you probably learned about in elementary school. The fruit today grows wild in all but the hottest and coldest regions of North America. Chokecherries have a strong astringent flavor, indicating a high level of tannins that is a welcome component in well-balanced wine.

The shrubs that bear chokecherries are best adapted to river and creek beds, but you can find them today in open fields, along roads and railroad tracks, and at the edges of woodlands. The plants reach about 8 feet tall and bloom in late spring. At the end of summer, the clusters of grape-size fruit ripen from dark red to deep purple/nearly black, becoming sweeter and a bit less astringent as they do. The fruit continues to ripen after it changes color, so wait a week or two after they darken before you pick them.

ELDERBERRIES belong to the genus *Sambucus*, and as you might guess, they are used to flavor the liqueur Sambuca, as well as St. Germain, another popular liqueur. Elderberries are also used to make a variety of natural remedies, especially those aimed at treating respiratory ailments. In the classic play and film *Arsenic and Old Lace*, a pair of spinsters murder men by serving them poisoned elderberry wine.

The American elderberry is a native plant found all over North America, and the European elder, which came here with settlers, has spread via birds to many uncultivated areas. They are especially abundant in wet areas, such as you find near lakes, swamps, and retention basins. The shrub grows 12 to 20 feet tall and opens its big, white, very fragrant flowers in late spring to early summer. The berries look a lot like blueberries, with skin that turns dark blue to black in late summer and early fall. (You may find varieties of red elderberries, but you want to pass on those. They're mildly toxic, though not lethal, and they just don't taste good.) Pick the berries when the skin is glossy and completely dark. Before you use them, remove all the stems and leaves—some find that it's easier to freeze the fruit clusters before you try to pull them from the stems.

MULBERRIES are found throughout the world. In North America you are most likely to find the native red species and the white mulberry that was brought here from Asia to feed silkworms and has since naturalized, or escaped into the wild. You may also come across black mulberry trees planted long ago and still thriving untended at old homesteads and cemeteries.

The soft berries look most like raspberries, though they tend to be a little bigger and softer. Red mulberries are pinkish red when unripe, but turn a darker red or even black when ripe. White mulberries are a pale, nearly white color when unripe, and turn red or deep pink as they mature. Mulberry trees typically grow 40 to 60 feet tall. The fruit ripens in late spring to early summer, and many berries drop to the ground as they mature. In fact, you are more likely to notice mulberries as a mess on the ground than on the tree. The best way to harvest the fragile fruit is to spread a sheet or tarp beneath the tree and shake the branches. The berries will fall easily and quickly fill up your sheet.

 HONEYSUCKLE is an aggressive vine that's banned in some states yet still for sale in others. Any place that's not regularly mowed—behind strip malls, between suburban subdivisions, abandoned lots—you're almost sure to find honeysuckle winding its way around anything vertical or spreading along the ground. You might never notice it except for a brief week or two in spring when the white-and-yellow flowers open and release the freshest, sweetest scent you can imagine.

The flowers are the only part of the honeysuckle you want. You may see the flower buds a week or two before they open, but you're sure to notice them when they do. The soft flowers are short-lived, both on the vine and in the bucket. Pick them as soon as you see them and use them as soon as you pick them. Don't pick the berries—they're poisonous.

DANDELIONS might be public enemy number one in the United States, if you consider how much homeowners spend each year to rid their lawns of the scourge. Just a few generations back, dandelions were valued as healthy greens for spring salads and as an ingredient for making wine. A resurgent interest in eating dandelions, though, has not slowed the sales for herbicides to kill them. In open fields and other places where you can be certain have not been treated with toxic chemicals, you can harvest an almost limitless supply of dandelions in spring and again in the fall.

You can harvest the green leaves in early spring (always leave a few behind) to enjoy in salads and remember to come back a few weeks later, on the first warm days of the season, to pick the bright yellow flowers for wine. The sooner you pick them, the better, as they lose their sweetness as they begin to turn into the puffy, white seed balls. They won't keep long after you pick them, either.

MAKING WINE

AMOUNT NEEDED (FOR 5 GALLONS OF WINE):

Chokecherries: 15 pounds

Elderberries: 10 pounds

Mulberries: 10 pounds

Honeysuckle: 6 quarts flowers

Dandelions: 6 quarts flower heads, packed

ADDITIONAL INGREDIENTS

Sugar: 10 to 11 pounds (least for berries and honeysuckle, most for
   chokecherries and dandelions)

Yeast nutrient: 1 to 2 tablespoons

Sliced lemons (two or three per 5 gallons of must), or 2 tablespoons acid blend

For chokecherries, elderberries, or mulberries: 1 to 2 teaspoons pectic enzyme

For honeysuckle or dandelions: strong black tea (1/2 cup per gallon of must),
   or 2 teaspoons wine tannins

PREPARATION

Chokecherries: Remove all stems and leaves you picked with the fruit and then place
the chokecherries in a large pot. Pour in enough water to barely cover them and simmer until the fruit is soft, which can take two to three hours. Strain the juice and pour it
into your primary fermentation bucket, and put the pulp into a nylon bag. Add more
water to get 5 gallons of fluid, then steep the bag of pulp in the water for twenty-four
hours. Stir in the sugar until it is fully dissolved, then add the sliced lemons, yeast
nutrient, pectic enzyme, and tea. Wait another twenty-four hours, remove the bag, and
squeeze it gently to extract the remaining juice, and compost the pulp. Pitch the yeast.

Elderberries: First, be aware that elderberry juice is a dark purplish color that stains
nearly everything it comes in contact with. Wear old clothes and a pair of gloves when
handling the fruit. Removing the stems is essential but can be challenging. Freezing
the berries first (place them on a tray in your freezer for a couple of hours) makes it easier for you to separate the fruit just by running your fingers against the stem. When

your berries are free of stems, put them in your primary fermentation bucket and pour in enough boiling water to just cover them. Leave to steep for twenty-four hours, then pour in more boiling water to get to 5 gallons. Stir in the sugar until it is dissolved and add the lemons, pectic enzyme, and yeast nutrient. Cover and wait another twenty-four hours. Pitch the yeast.

Mulberries: Like raspberries, mulberries are a soft fruit with pesky little seeds. After washing mulberries, put them in a nylon bag. Over the primary fermentation bucket, gently squeeze the bag to crush the berries, then pour a gallon of boiling water over the bag in the bucket and let it soak overnight. The following day, add more boiling water (enough to get you 5 gallons of fluid) and stir in the sugar, lemons, pectic enzyme, tea, and yeast nutrient. Cover and wait twenty-four hours, then remove the bag and gently squeeze it to extract any remaining juice. Compost the pulp. Pitch the yeast.

Honeysuckle or dandelions: The delicate blossoms of these plants begin to deteriorate almost the moment you pick them, so be ready to start making the must right after you gather them. Remove any stems or green parts, which will leave behind off-flavors in your wine. In a large pot, boil a couple of gallons of water, turn off the heat, and add the flowers. Cover and let sit for twelve to twenty-four hours. Bring the flower water to a simmer for an hour, then strain the liquid and pour it into a primary fermentation bucket. Stir in sugar until it is dissolved, then add enough more water to get to 5 gallons. Blend in the tea and yeast nutrient, float the lemon slices on top, and wait another twenty-four hours before pitching the yeast.

BEST YEAST: Montrachet Red (chokecherries, elderberries, or mulberries),
    Montrachet White (honeysuckle), and K1V-1116 (dandelion)
TIME TO FIRST RACK: Five to six days
TIME TO DRINK: Two years

⨯⨯⨯⨯⨯⨯⨯⨯⨯⨯⨯⨯⨯⨯ ALCOHOL LIMIT ⨯⨯⨯⨯⨯⨯⨯⨯⨯⨯⨯⨯⨯⨯

THE BALANCE BETWEEN ALCOHOL CONTENT AND FRUIT FLAVOR IS A FINE LINE that takes some practice to get right. The flavor of grapes is rich enough to come through when the ABV is 12 to 20 percent (less for white wines, more for dark reds and port). Wine made with other fruits and vegetables are overpowered by that concentration of alcohol, according to Robert Kime, a researcher at Cornell University. He found that when the ABV in fruit and vegetable wines exceeds 10.5 percent, the alcohol reacts with and dissolves flavor compounds in the wine. When your wine is at 10.5 ABV, you can abruptly end the fermentation by chilling the must to just-above-freezing temperatures.

SPOTLIGHT ON: FLORIDA ORANGE GROVE AND WINERY, ⨯⨯⨯⨯⨯⨯ SAINT PETERSBURG, FLORIDA ⨯⨯⨯⨯⨯⨯

THE IDEA STARTED WITH ORANGES, NO SURPRISE, AT THE FLORIDA ORANGE Grove and Winery in Saint Petersburg. "We were in the citrus business, selling oranges and juice, and we still had plenty of fruit, so we began thinking about what we could make with the oranges," recalls Vince Shook, the owner and winemaker. "The idea of making wine came up and when we looked into it, we found that just a few wineries offered citrus wines, and they were bad."

In 1991, Shook saw this opportunity and began to teach himself how to make wine. "I was trained as an engineer, so I looked at the winemaking process and took it apart, step by step, to adjust each variable to the benefit of orange juice," he says. "We went through a lot of trial and error, and by 1997, we had wines to share."

Shook was hooked on the process and began experimenting, first with other citrus fruits, such as tangerine, grapefruit, and Key lime; next with tropicals such as pineapple and mango; then berries and stone fruits; and now with carrots and tomatoes. For each ingredient, he needed to test different varietals, as well as tinkering with the sweetness, pH, alcohol level, and aging. "Once you are comfortable with the process of making wine," he says, "it's only five percent chemistry. The other ninety-five percent is art."

Today, the winery offers thirty-seven different varieties of wine. "Our goal is to capture the flavor of the fruit in the wine so that if you like raspberries, you will like the flavor of our raspberry wine," Shook says. For that reason, the single fruit and vegetable wines are not blended with grape juice. "We think that drinking our wines can be like a visit to the place where they were produced, that they have a distinct *terroir* just like any wine."

CHAPTER № 3

HOME BREWS

BEER IS THE MOST POPULAR ALCOHOLIC BEVERAGE IN THE UNITED States and a nearly $100 billion industry. The national annual per capita consumption of beer is about 21 gallons, which is a little more than half that of the Czech Republic, the world's beer-drinking leader. Beer became America's favorite drink only after the repeal of Prohibition in 1933, when standardization and mechanization made it cheaper to produce and distribute than hard cider and wine. Before long, beer had become another commodity in our industrial food system and the differences among the biggest brands came to be more about marketing and packaging than ingredients and flavor. The beer was almost all made in the pilsner style, which produces a pale yellow brew with a lightly bitter, sweet taste and low to moderately low alcohol content.

In the past thirty years, beer lovers have enjoyed the revival of craft beer, made in small batches with an emphasis on quality. Craft brewers have introduced drinkers to the many styles of beers and their unique characteristics. Home brewing, commonplace before Prohibition, never disappeared completely, but it was mostly the hobby of eccentrics, cheapskates, and homesteaders until microbrews sparked interest in making beer again. Today, the American Homebrewers Association reports that it has thirty thousand members and estimates that a million Americans are brewing at least one batch of beer for themselves each year. About 90 percent of professional brewers begin learning their craft at home, the group says.

Brewing your own beer couldn't be easier these days. In many areas you can go to a shop with all the supplies and equipment you need, and you can use it right there, even storing your beer there while it ferments. This is a low-risk way to learn about brewing. If you're ready to set out on your own, you can buy malt extracts, which greatly simplify the brewing process. Malt extracts are concentrated sugars from grains, the sugars that the yeast ferments into alcohol. Extracting those sugars yourself takes time, but not expensive equipment or extensive know-how, as you'll learn in this chapter. Growing the ingredients yourself takes even more time, but not a lot of effort for the reward of truly making your own beer from scratch. We'll begin with growing your own hops—because hops take less space and postharvest processing than raising grains, home brewers are more likely to start with them. If you'd like the bigger challenge and greater satisfaction of producing all of your own ingredients, I've included the basics of growing grains in a small patch and instructions on how to turn them into fermentable malt.

XXXXXXXXXXXXX GROWING HOPS XXXXXXXXXXXXX

Barley wine would be as close as we'd get to beer if not for the discovery of two very valuable properties of hops. The plant had long been used by traditional healers as a medicinal herb, most often as a mild sedative and pain reliever. About a thousand years ago, brewers began to realize that the resin in hops flowers is a natural preservative and thwarts the activity of microbes other than yeast. Equally important, brewers found that each variety of hops imparts a distinct bitter flavor and aroma that balances the sweetness of malt in beer, and that those characteristics are transformed by the boiling and fermentation process to create the many different styles of beer. Mead and cider makers also now use hops to add a dash of bitterness and preservatives to their recipes.

Hops, the plant botanists call *Humulus lupulus*, is a perennial, meaning it comes back in the same place every year. The aboveground growth dies in winter, but the roots survive and resprout the following season. Hops roots are known to continue producing new growth for fifty years and more, though fifteen years is more typical.

Each spring, the roots send up new bines (like vines, only they wrap around supports rather than latch on with tendrils, as true vines do) that can grow as much as 10 inches a day and eventually reach up to 25 feet tall. The plants are dioecious, which means there are separate males and females. The males' sole value is to pollinate the females, the source of all of the desirable acids and oils that preserve and flavor the beer. Whether or not they are pollinated, female plants bear small, conelike flowers in late summer, and the flowers contain the all-important flavor and aroma compounds.

Hops grow well throughout the temperate areas of North America, but not in the extreme north (the growing season is too short) or extreme south (not enough cold days). If you have a good spot for them, they are almost carefree.

VARIETALS

Of the dozens of varieties of hops, four are known as the noble hops, prized above all others for their rich aromas and flavors. The four varieties—Hallertau (or Hallertauer), Saaz, Spalt, and Tettnang—originated in the regions of Central Europe for which they are named. They are used extensively in commercial brewing and, like Champagne or Vidalia onions, they are considered authentic only if grown in their region of origin. That's because hops' characteristics change depending on where and how they're grown.

Each variety of hops has a unique balance of alpha and beta acids that impacts the beer's flavor and determines when in the brewing process is best to use them. The variations allow you to choose and grow a few that produce beer exactly to your taste. Most brews include two kinds of hops: those that are high in the bitter alpha acids, categorized as bittering hops, and those heavier in the aroma- and flavor-rich beta acids, referred to as finishing hops because they're used later in the process to create the taste you're aiming for.

You can grow the classic European varieties of hops in North America, but plant breeders have developed many new choices selected to produce reliable results in the conditions here. These are a few choices a novice can feel confident with. Plant both a bittering and a finishing variety, and you'll have all that you need to brew with. If you can only grow one, go with a finishing type because it has the most impact on your final results. A good one for most areas of North America is Cascade, developed at Oregon State University. Bred to resist downy mildew, a disease that can afflict hops in cool, damp climates, it is widely adapted and the easiest to grow successfully in the widest range of conditions. Its aroma is floral and citrusy. Many American pale ales and lagers are made with Cascade.

If you want to make an English-style ale, Fuggle and East Kent Golding are British varieties that fare well on this side of the Atlantic.

Centennial can be used both for bittering and adding aroma to the brew. It's a hybrid of several European varieties and it grows well throughout North America.

Nugget, an American variety with high alpha acid content, is used primarily for bittering. It is productive and tolerant of a broad range of conditions. Nugget is often used along with other varieties because it helps the beer foam properly—that's important because many of the aroma compounds are released in the foam.

Amarillo is a proprietary variety of Virgil Gamache Farms in Washington, so you have to buy the rhizomes, or starter roots, from one of its authorized distributors. It is valued for its aroma, which is both spicy and redolent of oranges. It's commonly used in the many India pale ales that have become popular in recent years.

Northern Brewer is a bittering variety that adds piney flavor to strong ales and stouts.

Tettnang is one of the noble hops that is best for growing in North America. If you want to make lagers or wheat beers, plant Tettnang.

Even if you don't grow hops for brewing, you might consider planting a few as a landscape plant that forms a dense screen for your yard. Golden hop vine (*Humulus lupulus aurea*) is a beautiful choice for that purpose.

SITE

Before you make a decision on where to plant hops, remember that it is a perennial that will come back year after year in that spot. You want to choose a site where you don't intend to plant other crops and where you won't have trees, shrubs, or other obstacles that will block sunlight from reaching the hops. The bines need lots of sunlight to produce the most aromatic and flavorful cones. The ideal location leaves them unshaded most, if not all, of the day during the growing season, which takes about four months.

Hops don't take up much ground space, but they can grow up to 25 feet tall each year, if you give them the support to get there. The site you choose needs to allow you to set up a trellis or other structure on which they can grow. Air circulation isn't as crucial with hops as it is with fruit trees, but the cones will be healthier if you can place them where breezes can dry dew and other moisture off of them, especially early in the day.

SOIL

Hops grow best in loose, sandy soil because drainage is very important to their overall health. They need a steady supply of nutrients, especially nitrogen, and water to grow those tall bines and they produce best where the soil pH is near neutral, though they can tolerate slightly acidic conditions. The best—really, only—way to add nutrients to sandy soil and neutralize the pH while keeping it well drained but not too dry is with compost. If you can, start adding a lot of compost to the soil in the autumn before you intend to plant hops. If you miss that window, start at least a couple of months before your last frost date in spring. You can just layer it on top of the soil or dig it into the first 6 inches or so.

Where the soil has more clay and doesn't drain well, the soil holds more nutrients but needs to be loosened. Again, the answer is compost. And again, starting as soon as the fall before you plant, dig down at least a foot—more if you can—and mix the soil with at least an equal amount of compost. Add more in the spring before you plant.

PLANTING

Hops grow from crowns, which include both rhizomes and true roots. Rhizomes are very similar to flower bulbs and potato tubers—a plump stem that grows relatively close to the soil surface (a few inches down) and puts out new shoots each spring. Rhizomes also produce new rhizomes, which you can harvest to increase your hops plot or share with others. (I'll explain how to do that on page 101.) The roots attached to the hops crown can grow as deep as 12 feet (yes, feet!) into the soil to help support and nourish those tall bines. A mature bine can produce about 2 pounds of hops each season.

The most efficient and productive way to plant hops is in clusters (sometimes called hills) of two crowns together with 3 feet or more between the clusters. After the last frost in spring, dig a hole a foot wide and about 6 inches deep. Place two crowns in the hole with their buds (little sproutlets like you see on potatoes that you have stored for too long) pointing up. Cover the crowns loosely with soil and water the area well, but take care not to drown the rhizomes by oversoaking the ground.

New hops plants devote nearly all of their energy to building their extensive root systems. That can leave room on the surface for weeds to move in and suck away vital moisture and nutrients from the hops. Clear away weeds before you plant hops and cover the soil with organic mulch such as dried grass clippings, shredded leaves, or straw (not hay) to obstruct new weeds from sprouting up.

Hop Vine Trellis

CARE

Like all new plants, hops crowns need to be kept consistently moist until they start to develop a deep root system. Do your best to prevent the soil from drying out through at least the first month or so of the first growing season. After the bines sprout up and begin growing, switch from daily light watering to soaking the soil weekly (or at most twice weekly). Whenever you irrigate your hops bines, direct the water flow to the soil rather than the leaves of the plant—wet foliage is the breeding ground of downy mildew and the other fungal diseases that are the only problems hops commonly suffer from.

In subsequent seasons, you can begin with deep watering once a week. As the growing season progresses and the cones begin to form, water the plants only during extended spells of drought. Dry conditions encourage the production of lupulin, the resin in the cones that contains the alpha and beta acids, the source of hops' aroma and flavor.

The first season after you've planted hops, the bines may reach only 6 to 8 feet tall and bear just a few cones as the plant builds its root structure. Don't fear that you've done something wrong or chosen an inhospitable location—the plants will become more vigorous the next year and yield an increasingly robust harvest each season. The rhizomes continue to remain vital and productive for fifteen years or more. When the bines do sprout up each spring and reach about a foot long, you have to choose from among the many shoots that each crown produces. Find the three that look the healthiest and most vigorous in each cluster and cut off the others. Be ruthless about this or you will end up with a tangled mess of bines and a diminished harvest of cones. Again, leave no more than three in each cluster.

Once you've settled on the two or three bines you are keeping, you need to set up a structure on which they can grow to their full size. Hops bines have fine, slightly prickly hairs that they use to cling to other surfaces as they grow up. Fences, clotheslines, wooden arbors, or other existing structures can work as a trellis for your hops. If you have none of these already in place where you are planting, you can hang thin rope or cord that the bines can climb using a basic eyehook attached to your house's eaves and a tent stake at the bottom to secure the cord. You can also easily create a simple trellis, using bamboo poles. Bamboo is light, inexpensive, and reusable for several seasons. Get three poles at least $^3/_4$ inch in diameter and 12 feet or more in length for each hops cluster. Push the stakes into the ground at an angle so that they meet near the top—you should have what looks like the frame for a tipi. Use a plastic zip tie—sold with plumbing and electrical supplies—to hold the three poles together. Guide the bines onto the bamboo poles and stand back. Within a few days, the bines will wrap themselves around the poles and begin heading for the sky.

To grow those lengthy bines, hops need a lot of nutrients to feed on. The compost you added to the soil is a healthy supply of nutrients for it to start on, but you need to supplement those during the growing season. After the plants come up, spread an inch or so of compost around the base of the plants and lightly scratch it into the soil. Every other week after that, use a liquid fish and seaweed fertilizer when you water (follow the package instructions about dilution rates). Stop using the fertilizer when the first flower cones appear.

Hops can be plagued by pests such as aphids and spider mites, but they are primarily a problem for growers with large hopyards (as extensive plantings are called). For home growers, diseases caused by fungus are more common. Downy mildew is the most prevalent of the diseases and it can spoil your harvest. It may start as soon as the shoots emerge in spring and you can't miss the symptoms. The infected shoots are stunted, brittle, and lighter in color than healthy shoots, with leaves that stay curled or are deformed. You may see gray or black spores on the undersides of infected leaves. Warm wet weather encourages the disease, which is spread by wind and splashing rain. As soon as you see infected shoots, cut them off and dispose of them (but not in compost you will later use on your hops). If the weather is very humid or rainy when the flowers form, they, too, can become afflicted with downy mildew, causing the cones to stop growing and turn brown before they fully mature. Bear in mind that every season's weather varies, but if you've lost your hops crop to downy mildew more than once, consider planting a highly resistant variety, such as Cascade and Willamette. You can also reduce the risk of fungal diseases by trimming off lateral branches and even the foliage on the bottom 4 feet of the plant—this eliminates the breeding ground for fungal spores that splash up from the soil. Let the foliage grow back at the end of the season so it can help produce nutrients (via photosynthesis) for the rhizome to store for the next spring's new growth.

HARVEST AND BEYOND

Hops bines continue their vigorous growth into midsummer and then begin their flowering process. When the bines reach their full height, they start to develop lateral branches, primarily on the top third of the plant. At the end of the lateral branches, or side arms, small flower buds called burrs form. They are about 1/4 inch in diameter and have spiky petals (hence the term *burrs* to describe them). As the burrs mature, the spiky petals fall off and smaller, softer petals replace them. The softer petals eventually close up and form a tight, green cone that hangs off the side arms.

Knowing the exact moment when the cones reach their peak of ripeness takes experience with the particular variety you are growing—each matures at a slightly different time based on its own predisposition and the conditions where you are growing. You can begin looking for signs of ripeness in late summer, around mid-August in most climates. As the cones near maturity, they become lighter in color, softer than in the fully green stage, and drier, almost papery. The petals closest to the branch holding the cone may even become slightly browned.

Pluck one or two cones when you see the majority of them starting to show those signs of ripeness. Squeeze the test cones gently to be sure they are soft and dry. As you do that, you should get a strong whiff of the bitter, resiny odor of the lupulin glands. The scent is distinctly bitter, potent enough that you may feel the impulse to turn your head away or pinch your nostrils closed. When the cones are fully dry and very aromatic, they are ready for harvesting.

Be sure all the cones are ripe before you harvest. Immature cones do not continue ripening and bulking up their flavor and aroma compounds once off the bine. Cones that have fully matured pluck easily from the side arms with just a gentle tug. When all of the cones are ripe, cut each bine down to about 3 feet high and harvest the cones from the cut bines. Wear gloves to protect your hands from the prickly bines.

A week or two of curing allows the cones to finish drying before you use and store them. Put them on an old window screen, grate, or other surface that allows air to circulate around them. You can do this outdoors or in, but be sure to keep the cones away from direct sunlight and any moisture. When they are dry almost to the point of crumbly, you can use them right away or store them in your freezer in a tightly sealed container or bag. Take the cones out of the freezer about twenty-four hours before you want to use them for brewing. If you've previously brewed with the hops pellets you get from many suppliers, keep in mind that you need to use a bit more of your homegrown crop than the dried form. As with herbs you use for cooking, dehydrating concentrates the aroma and flavor compounds, making them more potent than freshly picked plants. But what you lose in potency, you more than make up in the pure flavors you can only get from freshly picked, homegrown ingredients.

After the first hard outdoor freeze in late autumn or early winter, the remaining bines wither and turn brown. Cut them to ground level. To produce new rhizomes for your own use or to give away, start after the harvest by bending the bottom 3 feet of the bines to the ground and covering them lightly with soil and organic mulch. Over the winter and into early spring, the bines will grow roots at intervals along their buried stem. When the warm weather returns, uncover the stems and you'll see where they have swelled into the start of new rhizomes, each with an "eye," or pointed bud, preparing to sprout. Cut them apart with a sharp spade or pruning shears and then replant them like I described in the earlier section on planting (page 97).

GROWING BARLEY

Raising a small plot of your own grain adds another authentic layer to your homemade brew, and it's surprisingly easy to do. Even in a limited space, you can harvest enough barley to make a few special batches of beer. If you have lots of room, you can grow all of your own barley. You can also buy malted barley in small batches or in bulk to use in your own brew. But you have nothing to lose by trying to produce at least a little of your own—barley is the least demanding plant you'll ever grow.

VARIETALS

Barley is a versatile grain that's been cultivated for a variety of purposes. Hulled, or forage, barley is raised to feed cows and other livestock. Hull-less types become ingredients in soups, stews, and other foods for people. Malting barley is the kind used for brewing and you want to be sure that's what you get when you buy seeds or bagged barley.

There are two distinct species of barley: six-rowed and two-rowed. The names refer to how kernels line up on the plant's seed head. Those kernels are the grains that become malt for beer. The two species have a few other key differences. The six-rowed is more widely adapted and is especially suited to the East Coast and Midwest, and because it has a shorter growing season, the far North. Its grains are smaller and less starchy than the two-rowed kind, so you may need a bit more to get the same amount of malt. Robust is a reliable six-rowed barley you can find from many sources. Lacey is a very productive six-row. Expert brewers generally prefer the two-rowed types, which grows best where summers are not too humid, such as the Plains and the inland regions of the Pacific Northwest. Harrington is one of the most popular two-row malting barleys among craft and home brewers. Conlon, developed in North Dakota, is a two-row type that matures during short seasons.

If you live in a grain-growing region, diseases that affect barley may be more prevalent than they are in other areas of the country. Before you buy seed, ask nearby farmers or check with your local cooperative extension agent about the disease resistance you need to consider as you select a variety to plant.

SITE

All-day sun and well-draining soil is all that barley needs to thrive. How big is a sufficient size for a backyard barley plot? A 10-by-10-foot bed will produce up to 15 pounds of grain, if you sow densely, as if you were seeding a lawn. That's more than enough to make a 5-gallon batch of beer.

SOIL

Barley is not too fussy about the soil conditions—it grows vigorously even where fertility is low. It suffers poor germination and stunted growth where the soil is highly acidic, a pH below 6.0. If you've had a soil test that's determined your site is very acidic, you can remedy the problem by blending in a hefty dose of compost, which neutralizes the soil's pH level. Mix in the compost a month or two before you intend to plant and add more when you plant. If the soil test indicates low levels of phosphorus or potassium, blend in rock phosphates or greensand, two organic soil amendments, a month before planting.

If weeds are growing where you are planning to grow barley, take the time to pull or dig them all out—don't leave any roots behind or the weeds will grow back in the middle of your plot, where they will be difficult to get rid of. Right before you plant, use a spade or garden fork to loosen the top 6 inches of soil in your barley bed and water it until it's moist but not soaking.

PLANTING

Barley grows best in cool temperatures and needs about seventy days to fully mature. You can plant it in early spring, about six weeks before your last frost, or in late summer, if you live where you rarely get frost before November 1.

About $3/4$ pound of barley seed is enough to plant a 10-by-10-foot bed, from which you can harvest up to 15 pounds of barley. The seeds are very appetizing to birds, so plant a little more than you think you need because you will be sharing.

You can plant barley in orderly rows—leave at least 3 feet between each row so you can get in and manage any weeds that come up. Or you can just sow the seeds by scattering them on top of the loosened soil and count on the density of your barley stand to crowd out weeds that come up. If you choose the latter strategy, try to distribute the seed as evenly as possible so that you don't end up with thin or bare patches where

Barley in Orderly Rows

Barley Seeds Scattered

weeds can get established. Whichever approach you take, rake the soil lightly after you sow the seeds to cover them. Spread a layer of dried grass clippings, shredded leaves, or straw (not hay) to help keep the soil moist. The seeds will sprout in ten days to two weeks, depending on the air and soil temperature—germination takes a little longer in cooler conditions.

CARE

From the time you sow the seeds until they germinate and grow two sets of leaves, the soil in your barley plot needs to be consistently moist. If the soil is dry, sprinkle it lightly but don't soak it, which can drown the little seedlings. After the plants are established and growing steadily, you don't need to water them anymore, unless your area is hit by an extended spell of very hot and dry weather. In fact, barley needs no other attention from you while it's growing other than pulling any weeds that manage to sprout up in the patch. Try to get those weeds while they are small and have not yet had time to entangle their roots with the barley's, making it hard for you to remove them without collateral damage to your grain.

Barley, like many other grains, may fall over as it matures, which farmers refer to as lodging. This is caused by a variety of factors, including the variety's natural tendencies and heavy storms, but it is exacerbated by too much nitrogen in the soil. If you are tempted to use synthetic fertilizers to speed your barley's growth or bulk up its productivity, resist the urge. It's more likely to reduce your harvest because the weak stems that result won't be able to stand up when the seed heads (the source of the grains) are formed on top.

HARVEST

About three months after you plant barley—in midsummer if you started in early spring—the green stalks and the bristly seed heads on top begin to turn yellow and then brown. When they feel dry and brittle, the barley has matured and is ready to be harvested. Unless the weather forecast predicts an extended rainy spell—which can leave you with soggy grain that's hard to cull—don't rush to harvest the barley early. The riper it is, the easier the process of threshing is (more on that in a couple of paragraphs).

The traditional tool for harvesting grain by hand is a sickle, a cutting tool with a thin, sharp blade. You may still find those at barn sales and flea markets. If you don't have a sickle, you can use ordinary hedge shears. Either way, cut down the stalks to a couple of inches above the soil line.

As you're cutting the stalks, gather them into small bunches with all of the seed heads at the top. Tie the bunches together with twine and cut off all but 6 to 8 inches of the stalks. Put the bunches in paper grocery bags and store them in a cool, dry spot where they won't be raided right away by pests. Leave them for about two weeks, until the seed heads feel completely dry.

When they're dry, they're ready for threshing, or separating the grains you want from the other parts of the plant. To do this by hand, you can put the stalks on a sheet or tarp and whack them with a flail or broomstick until the grains come loose. You can also hold the stalks and beat the seed heads against the inside of a barrel or tub to shake the grains loose. If you like a neater approach, I've seen a home grain grower use a wooden frame with hardware cloth (a medium-mesh screen) stapled to it and set on

Threshing Grain by Hand

top of a tub or other container. When the seed heads are rubbed back and forth on the screen, the grains fall through the screen and into the tub. However you choose to harvest the grains, consider wearing garden gloves because barley has bristly "awns" attached to the seed head that can scratch your hands and the stalks splinter when they are dry. After threshing, you can use the leftover straw to mulch your garden or add it to your compost pile.

No matter how neat you are about threshing, you will have a pile of grains with chaff, or small bits of the plant, mixed in. Winnowing is the process of separating the grain from the chaff. A breezy day or a small fan makes winnowing easier. As you slowly pour the threshed grain from one container to another, the lightweight chaff blows away while the heavy grain falls into the container. You may find a few larger pieces of chaff have slipped through and into your grain—take the time to remove them by hand so they don't spoil your malt. Store your homegrown grain in a plastic or other airtight container with a lid—mice and other rodents are strongly attracted to stored grain, so you need to prevent them from noticing that you have it. Keep the container in a cool, dark place until you are ready to use it. Since you took the trouble to grow it, try to malt it while it is at its freshest, ideally within a week or so after threshing it.

One of the most valuable, and simplest, ways to improve your barley harvest each year is to save some of the seeds, which are the grains, from this season to plant next. If you set aside seeds from the sturdiest and most productive plants at harvest time and replant them the following season, each succeeding generation will be better adapted to the specific conditions in your yard. What you'll have is your own personal strain selected for your garden. You can even name your strain, if you like.

GRAIN ALTERNATIVES

Barley is the fundamental grain for beer, but brews made with half barley and half wheat have a long tradition in Europe and have become very popular here in recent years, especially for lighter drinking in summer. The conditions and soil in which wheat grows and the steps in the process for raising it in a small plot are nearly identical to those for barley. When selecting varieties, you have a choice between spring or winter wheat. Spring wheat is planted, like barley, a few weeks before the last frost in spring and is ready for harvest in midsummer. Winter wheat is planted in fall, grows a little before the first freeze sets in, then sits dormant (indifferent to the cold) until warm weather and long days return in spring. It finishes its growing season in mid-spring, around late April to early May in most climates. If your garden space is limited, planting winter wheat keeps your plot productive during a time of year when you aren't growing other crops. Harvest, thresh and winnow your small wheat crop just as you would barley.

Some of the most popular commercial brews are made with corn or rice to supplement the barley, because those grains are less expensive. They tend to make beer that's bland and not as full-bodied as brews from barley. You can grow those grains in small plots, but you need a sizable space to harvest enough even for a single batch of brew. For all of those reasons, they're not worth growing for your homegrown brews.

Oats and rye, used in some unique brews, are easy and even productive enough to grow in a garden. In fact, you should because they are very helpful "green manure" crops that increase the fertility and enhance the texture of your soil. You grow them just as I described for barley. However, they are more difficult to extract enough sugar from. If you do decide to grow them, use them as just a small portion of the grain in your brew—no more than 25 percent of the total—to be sure you get enough sugar and enzymes in the wort.

MALTING, MASHING, AND SPARGING

Although they sound to me like the name of a British law firm, the terms *malting*, *mashing*, and *sparging* refer to the process of converting the starches in grains into a sugary liquid you can ferment.

The first step is malting, or germinating the grains to activate the enzymes inside that help transform starch, which the seed would use for food when you plant it, into sugar. To begin, weigh the grains and take note of the amount, as it will help you to know this information a few steps later in the process. As a rule of thumb, you need about 2 pounds of raw grain for each gallon of homemade brew you plan to make.

After weighing, rinse the grains thoroughly and remove any remaining chaff, which floats to the top. Drain the rinse water away and then put the grains in a plastic container with a lid. Add enough water to cover the grains by 2 inches. Put on the lid and let the container sit away from heat and direct light for two hours. Drain the water and let the grains sit and dry with no lid for about eight hours. Don't forget and leave the grains in water too long or they will drown, never to be useful for brewing. Check the grains to see if the tips have developed whitish bulges where the rootlet known as the acrospire will emerge. If you see the bulge, you can move to the next step; if you don't, repeat the soak and drying cycle again, and even a third time, if necessary, until the grains are bulging at one end.

When the grains do have the telltale bulge, they're ready to germinate and become malt. Spread them in a single layer on large baking sheets or other flat trays—professional brewers use a dedicated malting floor for this. (If you don't have enough trays for all the grain you want to malt, you can do several batches in stages and just keep the batches that are finished in a plastic container with a lid.) Cover the trays with plastic to trap humidity and keep debris and pests away from the grain. Dry cleaner bags work well for this; you can also use trash bags or even plastic wrap. Put the trays in a spot where the temperature stays between 60° and 75°F and they are shielded from direct sunlight. In warmer temperatures they're likely to develop mildew before they sprout.

Gently turn the grains each day with a spatula and mist them with water if they are dry. In four to six days, the acrospires will have sprouted from the grains and begun growing. Starting on the fourth day, watch them closely and note when the vast majority of the acrospires are about as long as a grain. At that point, you have malted barley that's ready for drying.

To stop the grains from germinating and transform them from green malt into the flavorful malts needed for brewing, they are dried in a kiln set at a very low temperature. You probably don't have a kiln, so instead you can use a standard food dehydrator (often found used at yard sales and swap meets) or you can dry your malted grain in an ordinary oven, if you can keep the temperature between 90° and 120°F. (The pilot light of a gas oven keeps it around 90°F when the oven is turned off.) You may also find spots with that temperature around your home, such as on top of a gas hot water heater or another appliance. Wherever you find your warm spot, spread the grain again in a single layer and let it dry for twenty-four hours, turning it often to ensure the kernels all dry evenly. To give the malt a richer flavor, raise the temperature to 140° to 150°F to lightly toast the grain for the last two hours. When ready, the barley grains will be crunchy and taste lightly sweet. Stifle any urge you have to dry the grains faster by raising the temperature early—too much heat neutralizes enzymes in the grains that play a vital role in the process of converting starch to sugar. Weigh the grain again—it should be within an ounce of the same weight as when you started, with the added rootlets compensating for the moisture loss that occurred during drying. (If the grain weighs more, it is not dry enough. Give it another twenty-four hours of drying in the 90° to 120°F range and weigh it again.) After weighing, pour the grain into a colander and shake gently to loosen and separate the rootlets from the grain. Sift through the grain with your fingers to cull out the rootlets. You can store dry grain for a couple of weeks in a sealed container.

The barley is now pale malt, the primary ingredient for any beer. At this point, you can move to the mashing process. If, however, you want to turn some of the pale malt into crystal, amber or brown malts used to make darker beers, you can continue to roast the malted barley in your oven. Toast the grains for an hour at 212°F to make crystal malt, which adds sweetness and color to your brew. Raise the temperature to 350°F and shorten the toasting time to fifteen to twenty minutes to make amber malt. Leave the malt at that temperature for thirty minutes to make brown malt. Be aware that toasting the darker malts can produce a lot of smoke. If you don't have great ventilation in your kitchen, you can toast the grains on an outdoor grill, but be sure to keep them from sitting over direct flames, which can cause charring, a flavor you don't want to taste in your homemade brew. Once you've malted your own grain, you can call yourself a maltster, which is a real term even though it sounds like I made it up.

Mashing lets the enzymes in the malted grain convert starches to sugars. You capture the sugars in wort, the sweet malt tea that you ferment to make beer. There are several ways to do this, but the easiest for home brewers (especially novices to all-grain brewing) with limited gear is the single infusion method. I'll explain that, and when you're more experienced and better equipped you can explore the more complex step-mashing and decoction methods.

You start by cracking the malted grain. You can find malt mills scaled for home brewers that cost about $100 to $150 for a hand-cranked model to more than $200 for motorized versions. For your first few batches, you can crack the grains by running them over with a rolling pin on a sturdy, flat surface. Be careful not to press too hard—

you don't want to crush the grain, just to break open the husk so water can get to the starch inside.

One piece of equipment you need to mash your malted grain is a mash tun, also called a lauter tun. It is a large (typically 10-gallon) jug with a grated false bottom on which the grains rest, piping to help keep the fluid at a steady temperature, and valves through which the sweetened water runs. If you're adept with a welder and plumbing supplies, you can find designs for making your own from a large plastic water cooler or you can buy one online for about $120.

The single-infusion process is not complicated, but you do want to pay attention to the temperature of the water you use and timing to maximize the activity of the enzymes that convert the starches to sugar. Heat to 168°F 1 quart of water for each pound of grain you are using. (You need about 12 pounds of grain to make 5 gallons of beer.) Add water and then grain to the tun and check the temperature. It should settle to 154°F in about ten minutes. You can adjust, if necessary, by adding a small amount of hotter or colder water. When the temperature holds at 154°F, the various enzymes in the grain go to work and begin breaking down the starches. Put a lid on the tun and wait forty-five minutes for the water to infuse with the sugars.

A simple iodine test tells you when the starches have turned to sugar. To do it, fill a small dish with a sample of your wort and add a couple of drops of ordinary iodine. It turns dark blue to black when the starches have not been fully converted to sugar. If you get that reading, keep the water at 154°F and continue to test at five-minute intervals. The iodine stays its normal brown color in a solution of sugar only.

Sparging is the technical term for rinsing the grains to capture the maximum amount of sugar from them when the mashing is done. As you get near the end of the forty-five minute infusion, you want to heat more water to 180°F. The grains absorb some of the water you started with. The fresh hot water captures the sugars in the tun and becomes the foundation of your brew. You need enough of the fresh hot water to leave you with 5 gallons of fluid at the end of the rinsing.

When the mashing period is done, slowly pour the hot water into your tun and gradually drain out the liquid through the attached valve. Let it run into a brew kettle, a large stockpot with a lid you will use to boil the wort before fermenting it. The first quart or so of fluid to come out of the tun may be cloudy or have bits of grain husk in them. Pour it back in at the top of the tun and continue adding the hot water. Be patient

Sparging Grain

and allow all of the liquid to flow out of the tun before you add fresh hot water, 2 quarts at a time. After adding the water, stir it gently for a few minutes. You may need as long as forty minutes to capture 5 gallons of the sugar-rich liquid. The more sugary the liquid, the more raw material you have for the yeast to convert to alcohol, so you don't want to rush this step. Once you have collected 5 gallons of malt sugar, your home-grown malted, mashed, and sparged wort is ready for you to brew into beer. When the mash tun cools, toss the spent barley grains into your compost pile, where they can be recycled back into nutrients for next year's crop. You can also feed the spent grains to chickens; if you don't have chickens of your own, you may be able to swap them for eggs with someone who does. Spent barley is easy to turn into flour for baking—find out more about that in "Grains to Goodies" on the next page.

THE BOIL

After you've turned your homegrown malt into the sweet grain tea, called the wort, you can begin brewing with it. For all the varieties of beer, the basic steps are simple. The differences come as you adjust the details, from malt, yeast, and hops selections to temperature and timing for the type of beer you'd like to brew. You can prepare the wort for fermentation in a few hours with just a few additional pieces of gear than you need for wine, mead, or cider. Your freshly made wort is, however, a cauldron of microbes eager to consume the sugars in it. Before you can put yeast to work ferment- ing it, you boil it to kill off the competition from the microbes. The boiling process also is the time to add the other key flavor component, hops.

The term *grain bill* is commonly used by brewers to refer to the mix of malts used in creating the beer. The basic ingredient in nearly every type of beer is pale malt, the simple malted barley. Pilsner is brewed with just pale malt. Other malts are added to the grain bill to make porters, stouts, wheat beers, and other specialty brews. I want to emphasize what many brewers told me about using homemade malt for the first few times—keep it simple. Choose a basic style of beer and make pale malt no less than half of your grain bill. Include no more than two types of malt (even barley malts such as crystal or amber) in your wort until you are very experienced in working with them. Also, homemade malts tend to have a lower concentration of active enzymes than do malt extracts and commercially produced all-grain malts. Use about a third more homemade malt in your brew when working from a recipe that is measured for commercial malts.

If you've sparged the grain as I described in the previous section, you have a large pot full of wort. The stockpot should be large enough to hold at least 6 gallons (so it doesn't boil over); larger pots are even better. You can use an ordinary kitchen stockpot with a lid, but a brew kettle, which has a spout at the bottom, makes the process easier and neater. You can find a new model, made of easy-to clean stainless steel, for about $70 (and a used one for less).

Put the potful of wort on the stove and heat it to a rolling boil. Don't walk away from it: for twenty minutes after the wort begins to boil it produces a lot of foam that quickly can spill over the sides. For that moment and others along the way, I've met brewers who use propane burners (such as those from the turkey fryers that have become so popular in recent years) to boil their wort outside. Wherever you boil, stay close by to keep an eye on the wort you worked hard to make. Leave the lid off the pot at this stage to reduce the risk of the boiling wort's spilling over. Also, during mashing and boiling, the malt produces a compound called dimethylsulfide that can make your beer smell and taste like corn or, even worse, rotting cabbage. It vaporizes when the wort boils and you don't want a lid to trap it and let it condense back in the brew. The higher the temperature of the wort, the more of the dimethylsulfide boils off. That's why experienced brewers recommend a consistent, rolling boil for the wort, not a slow simmer.

As the wort first reaches a steady boil, you can add bittering hops, such as Nugget, Galena, or Northern Brewer. You need about an ounce of hops for 5 gallons of wort. Simply float the hops cones in the wort. After a few minutes, you will smell the hops aroma, which mostly boils off. Maintain the wort at a rolling boil for a total of sixty minutes. As it boils, you may notice clumps forming in the wort. These are coagulated proteins and they can leave behind a haze in your finished beer and cause it to turn stale in the bottle. Even worse, those proteins can scorch if they sink to the bottom of your kettle during boiling and create burnt flavors. Stir the wort as it boils to prevent the protein clumps from forming.

After thirty minutes, the wort is ready for you to add finishing hops. These varieties have a high concentration of beta acids, and noticeable flavors and fragrances that are often described as spicy, herbal, floral, or even citrusy. Cascade, Fuggle, Willamette, and the many variations of the Golding strain available are all easy to work with varieties, each with unique flavor characteristics. Add an ounce of any variety of finishing hops to 5 gallons of wort.

If you like beer with a very strong hops flavor and aroma, add another 1/2 ounce or so about five minutes before the boiling hour is over. No matter how hoppy you want the beer to be, don't overdo the amounts at this stage—you will have another opportunity to add more "hoppiness" a few steps later in the process. As with the bitter hops, simply float the cones in the wort.

THE BIG CHILL

Boiling wort is too hot to host the microbes that compete with yeast and cause spoilage, but it's also not hospitable to yeast. Most strains flourish at temperatures below 75°F, and some (such as those that make lager) need conditions as low as 50°F to perform at their best. However, as soon as the wort begins to cool, troublesome bacteria naturally present in the air can move in. The more time between the end of the boiling and the pitching of the yeast, the more opportunity there is for unwanted bacteria to establish itself and ruin your brew.

To keep that interval as short as possible, you want to cool the wort to yeast-pitching temperatures as quickly as you can. Immersion chillers, which sell for $70 to $150, are coils of copper tubing filled with cool water that sit in the brew kettle. They're very efficient at rapidly cooling the wort to exactly the temperature you want. It's not hard to make your own chiller if you are handy, but you don't need an immersion chiller to quickly cool a 5- to 10-gallon kettle full of hot wort. Before you finish boiling, fill a large sink, laundry tub, or picnic cooler with ice water and have more ice on hand to add when the initial batch in the sink melts. As soon as you turn off the heat, put the lid on your kettle and shift it into the ice bath. Be ready to replace the ice when the water has been warmed by the kettle full of just-boiled liquid.

Cooling the wort to room temperature in an ice bath can take thirty minutes or more after you turn off the heat. You can stir the fluid to help move as much of it as possible into contact with rapidly cooling metal sides, but you need to be sure the spoon, your hands, and anything else that might come in contact with the wort is sanitized or you risk contaminating it with damaging microbes. A handmade brewer's cooling technique is to sanitize (outside and in) a used plastic soda bottle or other container and fill it with water, then freezing it. When you're ready to cool your wort, you plunge the frozen bottle into the kettle. Again, try this approach only if you are rigorous about sanitizing (and you should be).

A floating thermometer is the most reliable way to know exactly when the wort's temperature drops to room temperature, but you can be fairly sure when it feels cool to the touch—scoop out sample with a (sanitized) spoon rather than touch it with your finger. As soon as it's cool enough, pour the wort into your primary fermenter through a strainer to keep the hops and other debris out. Splashing as you pour adds oxygen for the yeast to grow on. If you're using a carboy, you can give it a gentle shake after pouring, for even more oxygen. Stir the wort, if you're brewing in a bucket.

WORT INTO BREW

Yeast is the third player in the preservation of your homegrown grains and hops. Dozens of different strains of brewing yeasts yield the wide variety of beers styles. Ale yeasts perform best in the range of 65° to 75°F, lager yeasts fare better in cooler conditions, generally lower than 60°F. When choosing a brewing recipe, consider the temperature of the room where you will store the fermenting wort. Most home brewers make ales because they don't have a spot cool enough for lager yeasts. Keep the temperature at a constant level wherever that may be.

As soon as your wort is at room temperature, take a hydrometer reading and write down the original (or starting) gravity. As I explained on page 23, you need that information to determine your beer's alcohol content. One standard package (10 grams) of dry or liquid yeast is enough to ferment 5 gallons of wort into pale ale. If your starting gravity is high, use a second package of yeast to ensure all of sugars are consumed. Pitch the yeast, set the airlock and let fermentation begin. How long that lasts depends on the yeast strain and the complex soup of ingredients—sugars, enzymes, proteins—in the wort, but you can expect after the initial lag time to see at least four days and no more than two weeks of vigorous bubbling and even a bit of swirling in the fermenter.

In the early stages of fermentation, foamy sediment (called krausen) forms at the top of the wort. When the yeast activity reaches its peak, some of the foam can be forced into the airlock. Keep the airlock clean and clear by removing it, rinsing it, and returning it quickly. Within a few days, the foam settles back into the beer and leaves the sediment adhered to the edges of the container. Shortly after, the fermentation slows and you have another opportunity to add more hops—again, just float them in the wort. Experienced brewers recommend you try adding at this stage only after you've brewed a few batches and know how the homegrown cones work for your tastes. Hops additions near the end of fermentation are very potent.

You can tell the fermentation has been successful when the beer is clear and has a rich, full color. If it's murky, give it a little more time. (Exception: You are trying to brew a yeasty, cloudy beer, such as a Belgian-style ale.) You may still see occasional bubbles in the airlock, indicating that some yeast continue to be active. During this phase, yeast turns some of its appetite on the by-products of fermentation, such as ketones and fusel alcohols, that leave behind funky tastes in your brew. You want to give this process as much time to play out as possible, but you don't want to leave the beer sitting with the spent yeast, hops, and other sediment for more than three weeks. About two weeks after you've pitched the yeast, take a hydrometer reading and compare it to your starting gravity. Take another reading the following day and the next. When your readings are constant for three days in a row, the beer is ready for bottling.

Being ready for bottling, though, is not the same being ready for drinking. The brew may be tasty, but it is flat. To create natural carbonation, mix it in a bucket with dextrose or another kind of priming sugar (dissolved in water) before you bottle it. (You'll find more details about priming sugar on page 38.) You need about $^2/_3$ cup of sugar for 5 gallons of brew—an amount that won't raise the alcohol content significantly, but will stimulate the yeast to make just a bit more carbon dioxide, the bubbles in your beer. Leave an inch of headspace at the top of your bottles before you cap them, to keep the pressure of the CO_2 from blowing the lids.

Beer doesn't need aging like wine, mead, and cider, but give it at least a couple of weeks to condition, or carbonate, in the bottle at room temperature before you taste it.

Then you can chill it in the refrigerator and get ready to taste what you made yourself, from seed to refreshing quaff.

HOMEGROWN FLAVORS

Beers flavored with fruit, herbs, and other natural ingredients can be a fun change of pace from your everyday ale. You can add homegrown berries, orchard fruit, or aromatics to your brew to create truly one-of-a-kind drinks.

FRUIT-FLAVORED BEERS are a Belgian tradition that has become popular in North America, especially in summer. You can use everything from peaches and strawberries to mangoes and bananas. When using real fruit—not extracts—you'll have the best results with raspberries, blackberries, tart cherries, and apricots. After rinsing your fresh-picked fruit well, freeze it overnight to kill microbes it's carrying and to begin breaking down the cellulose so it will release as much of its juice as possible. Partially thaw it for half an hour before using it. To get the most fruit flavor in your beer, puree it or put it in a nylon bag and crush it into the wort. Start with about 3 pounds of fruit for a 5-gallon batch of beer. If you really love the flavor, you can use as much as a pound of fruit per gallon.

While you're adjusting the amount of fruit to your taste, consider also your use of hops. You don't want the stronger flavors and aromas of hops to overwhelm the fruit, so try reducing or even eliminating the addition of aroma hops at the end of the boil.

When fruit is heated it releases pectin, molecules with a tendency to clump the pulp (which is why they're essential to making jam). Pectin makes beer look hazy. Adding fruit to the wort while it's boiling stimulates pectin production. During primary fermentation, you want the yeast to concentrate its energies on the maltose (malt sugar) and not be distracted by the fruit sugars, which will produce wine flavors. The best time to add fruit to flavor your beer is during a secondary fermentation in a carboy instead of bottling the beer when it's done the most active period. Add the pureed or crushed fruit to the container first, then rack the beer onto it. Gently swirl the carboy daily to help its flavor permeate all of the beer. Let the fruit infuse the beer for no less than a week and allow at least a few more days, if needed, for the pulp and other debris to settle before you bottle it.

HERBS AND SPICES, used judiciously, can help you create truly unique brews. Coriander, the seeds of the cilantro plants, is popular in wheat beer for its light citrusy flavor. About an ounce of the crushed seeds in a 5-gallon batch of brew is enough. Sage, parsley, and thyme are aromatic herbs that can give a brew a fresh, springlike flavor. Rosemary smells and tastes like pine resin, and may be substituted for some of the hops. You can experiment with adding herbs near the end of the wort boil, but the safest time to add them is in a secondary fermentation. (For information on growing herbs, go to page 180.) Start with $\frac{1}{2}$ ounce of herbs and add more than that in $\frac{1}{2}$ ounce increments if you want a stronger flavor in future batches.

SPRUCE was used in beer in the time before hops use became standardized, and spruce beer was still a common drink even into the eighteenth century. Today, spruce trees are a common landscape plant in many places. The new green shoots that the tree puts on each spring have, like hops and rosemary, a fresh, foresty scent. You can clip off the youngest, most tender tips from the spruce tree and add them to the wort at the end of the boil. To keep your brew from tasting too much like a Christmas tree, skip the addition of aroma hops when flavoring with spruce.

GINGER BEER

The ginger ale of my childhood—used in Shirley Temples with maraschino cherry juice—is more soda pop than fermented drink. My mother urged me to sip ginger ale when I complained of an upset stomach. Ginger does have a long history as a traditional remedy for digestive disorders. Fresh ginger also makes a spunky flavoring ingredient in a sweet, lightly alcoholic brew that you can drink alone or use as a base for real cocktails.

Ginger is a tropical plant that you can grow outside in the regions along the Gulf Coast and in containers you bring inside during cold weather just about everywhere else. The plant is a reedy perennial that in its native climate grows 3 to 4 feet tall and produces white and pink flower buds, which eventually open to yellow blooms.

GROWING GINGER

Ginger plants grow from rhizomes, the gnarly looking roots that you use to flavor stir-fries, baked goods, and cocktails. You can get different varieties, including variegated types, from nurseries specializing in tropical plants. Or you can just plant the rhizomes from ginger root you've purchased. If you do, choose roots that are shiny, plump, and have several little nubs (or sprouts) on them. Avoid any that look shriveled or feels soft—those have been sitting too long on the shelf to start growing vigorously again.

Heat and moisture are essential for ginger, but it grows best in light shade rather than in full sunlight. It can take morning sun, but direct afternoon sunlight tends to brown the leaves. The soil—in the ground or in a container—needs to be loose and very well-drained. Sandy soil is the norm in the semitropical regions of the United States, where ginger can be outside year-round. Mix in a shovelful of compost into each hole before you plant ginger, to increase the soil's fertility and help it steadily disperse moisture to the roots. Leave about 6 to 8 inches between each plant.

To grow ginger in a container, choose a pot that holds at least 3 gallons (5 gallons is even better). Make a blend of two-thirds peat or coir (coconut fiber) and one-third well-aged compost, with vermiculite sprinkled in. Fill the container up to about three-quarters with this blend and reserve the remainder to add later.

Spring is the best time to plant ginger outdoors or in. Start by soaking store-bought ginger in water for a few hours before you plant it, to wash off any antisprouting agents it was treated with. A healthy ginger rhizome typically has several sets of sprouts. To grow several plants, you can cut it into pieces, each of which has at least two sets. Place each piece on top of the soil in a pot and cover lightly—no more than 2 inches deep—with your soil mix. Water well and keep consistently moist. Setting the pot on a dish with pebbles and water can help maintain the constant humid conditions the plant thrives in. You also can use a spray bottle to mist it daily, especially helpful in the dry conditions found in most houses during winter. Ginger in containers can stay outside all the time through the months when the nighttime temperatures are warmer than about 55°F. Bring the containers inside after dark in spring and fall, and leave them indoors near a sunny window in winter.

Ginger is a slow grower, so you may not see much happening for a month or even more after you plant it. Don't worry, just keep it moist but be sure not to drown the roots by letting the soil become soggy. As the plant's stems grow, add more soil mix to the pot, but stop when the roots are about 4 inches deep. Once the stalks are up and growing, continue to keep them moist—remember, it's a tropical plant that thrives on humidity.

About five months after planting, the plant will be close at its full size and you can harvest some of the root to use for eating and brewing, if you want. Just scrape back enough soil so that the rhizome is exposed and cut off a piece to use. To harvest whole roots, wait until the aboveground foliage turns yellow and dies back, typically about nine to twelve months after you planted them. Turn over the pot, dig out the rhizomes with your hands and clip off any stalks still attached to them. Brush any dirt off but don't wash them. Put them in a cool, dry place away from direct sunlight for a couple of weeks and then get ready to use the juiciest ginger you've ever had. Set aside a few of the plumpest rhizomes (with sprouting nubs) to replant for your next batch of ginger.

BREWING WITH GINGER

START WITH GINGER JUICE. Powdered ginger works for brewing ginger beer, but since you've grown and harvested your own fresh roots, it's worth the effort to extract the juice directly. Grate the ginger roughly—you don't need to turn it into powder. Put the grated ginger in a fine-mesh strainer over a bowl and press on it with a spoon to squeeze out the liquid it contains. You'll be surprised how much there is in your home-grown ginger. After you've wrung all the juice out of the ginger, cook with or compost what's left in the strainer. You need about $1/2$ cup of ginger juice per quart of water to make ginger beer.

MAKE A SIMPLE SYRUP. Bring 2 quarts of water to a boil and thoroughly dissolve a cup of granulated sugar in it.

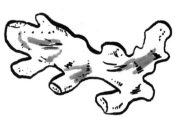

BLEND THE INGREDIENTS. Reduce the heat to low, then mix in the ginger juice, the juice from one lemon, and an ingredient that ginger beer enthusiasts insist is critical to a smooth, palatable flavor—cream of tartar. Add $^1/_2$ teaspoon to the 2 quarts of water.

PITCH THE YEAST. Allow the liquid to cool to room temperature and pour it into a fermentation bucket or just a large mixing bowl. Champagne yeast works well with these ingredients, but you can try other strains recommended for making white wine or cider. After pitching the yeast, put a lid on the bucket or cover the bowl with a towel. Wait twenty-four hours for fermentation to begin.

BOTTLE YOUR BREW. A day after you've pitched the yeast, pour the now fizzy liquid into bottles, leaving $^1/_2$ inch of headspace at the top, to allow room for the carbon dioxide produced by fermentation room to escape the fluid without blowing off the lid. Cap the bottles and store them in a cool, dark place. As I alluded to, ginger beer is prone to popping lids while it ferments, so put the bottles where potential collateral damage will be minimal.

STOP AFTER THREE DAYS. Allow fermentation to continue in the bottles for three days, then shut it down by putting them in your refrigerator for a couple more days. The alcohol content will be low—around 0.5 percent ABV—but definitely noticeable in the taste, if not in a buzz.

DRINK OR MIX. Aging does not improve the flavor of ginger beer; in fact, it begins to deteriorate after a week or so. Open the bottles carefully and enjoy your quick-brewed ginger beer no more than seven days after you put it in the refrigerator. Drink it by itself or make a traditional Jamaican Dark and Stormy cocktail by blending it with dark rum.

✕✕✕✕✕✕✕✕✕✕✕✕ THE BACKSTORY: BEER ✕✕✕✕✕✕✕✕✕✕✕✕

BEER BREWING BEGAN AT LEAST AS EARLY AS THE FIRST CIVILIZATIONS MADE the leap from gathering plants to growing them intentionally. The ancient Sumerians, the first people to leave behind written communication that can be understood today, paid their respects to a goddess of beer, Ninkasi. Wine and other drinks became important in the Mediterranean cultures that came along later, including the Greeks and Romans, but beer making became embedded in the cultures of the Germanic tribes of Northern and Central Europe, where the climate is less hospitable to wine grapes.

Almost five hundred years ago, in 1516, the prince of Bavaria decreed that beer could contain only three ingredients—water, barley, and hops. At the time, the role of yeast in fermentation and where yeast came from were not understood, even by experienced brewers. They relied on "starters" from previous batches to initiate fermentation with each fresh batch. The decree standardized beer making in Germany and Central Europe, but brewers in Belgium, the United Kingdom, and other cultures continued to create their own unique styles of beer with a variety of different grains and adjunct ingredients.

Brewing was a critical function even among the fun-averse Puritans in North America. Women brewed beer for their families to ensure a healthy supply of drink at a time when water purity was questionable. Home and small-batch brewing remained an essential to American life until the Prohibition laws banned it in 1919. Of course, Prohibition didn't end brewing any more than it eliminated liquor distilling. It just drove it underground and into the domain of organized crime.

Long after Prohibition was repealed, a federal law was passed in 1978 finally exempting home brewers from paying taxes on beer produced for personal consumption. Within a few months, the American Homebrewers Association was founded and competitions were launched. Today, only Alabama and Mississippi still prohibit home brewing. You can now participate in more than three hundred different amateur brewing competitions in North America.

CHAPTER 4

CIDER WITH A KICK

FOR AMERICANS, THE WORD *CIDER* USUALLY CONJURES UP MEMORIES of crisp fall air and the sweet, brownish, and thick juice from pressed apples. Tasty stuff for the family Halloween party, but it's just the raw material for what can become a drink that will bloom with complex flavors and a light, very pleasant amount of alcohol. Hard cider, as it's come to be known in the United States, is a fermented drink that generally ranges from 4 to 6 percent alcohol and may be still (like wine) or carbonated (like champagne). And like fermented grapes, cider becomes richer in complex flavors as it ages. Making cider is a simple and reliable way to preserve the rich taste of apples to enjoy any time of year. Pears and cherries also make great cider, alone or in blends with apples.

Hard cider was the most widely available and popular alcoholic beverage in America until Prohibition. In fact, it was the commonly consumed drink of any kind, because before municipal water systems many people did not have regular access to clean, potable water, making cider a safer choice. Most rural families and many city people made their own cider and enjoyed it as a daily refreshment. Our founding fathers reportedly drank tankards of cider with their morning and midday meals.

During and right after Prohibition, beer supplanted hard cider as the most popular drink and inexpensive wines proliferated and became the choice of those who like their drinks sweeter than beer. Cider became a seasonal type of rough-hewn apple juice. Today, hard cider is enjoying a revival, not only mass-produced and sold in six-packs by the major brewers and spirits companies, but also crafted by artisans and paired with food in the same way fine wine and beer are enjoyed. And it's no wonder. Real fine cider is a dry, effervescent, yeasty brew with a soft, delicate fruity aroma and flavor.

You can grow grapes just about anywhere in North America, but the varieties that produce the finest wine thrive in only a few regions. Apples are not native to the continent—they were brought here by the earliest settlers from Europe—but they have flourished and are adapted everywhere but the southernmost states.

Growing apples takes more patience than land. The trees can be less than 20 feet tall, so they fit into suburban yards and even airy city lots. (Bonus: They look and smell so enchanting when they bloom that you'll appreciate them in spring as much as you do when you pick the fruit.) But you do have to wait at least five years from the time you plant until you start harvesting your own apples. While you wait, you can skip to the cider-making section and practice making batches of cider with apples or cider you buy from local orchards.

VARIETALS

Any old apples will make cider, but as with grapes some varieties have been selected and bred for their cider-making qualities. The best-tasting ciders have a balance of acidic, astringent, and sweet flavors, so they're typically made with a blend of apples. Cider apples that are high in tannins (which produce astringent flavors) are categorized as bittersweet or bittersharp; those low in tannins are either sharp or sweet. A blend of varieties from those categories tends to produce the best-tasting cider, and gives you the chance to create a flavor that you like best. Traditional European cider varieties are increasingly available in the United States, and new ones developed at Washington State, Cornell, Minnesota, and other universities, along with regional nurseries, offer lots of options adapted to the diverse climate conditions in North America.

Apples, like many fruit trees, need a chilling time, which is winter dormancy caused by persistent exposure to cool temperatures. Without this chilling time, apple trees will stop growing, blossoming, and fruiting. The chilling times vary from one variety to another, but climates such as those in South Florida or along the Gulf Coast do not provide enough chilling time for nearly any apple.

Not to get you too involved in the sex lives of apple trees, but most varieties need a partner for pollination and even the so-called self-pollinators produce more fruit when grown near other apple trees. You'll get the best harvest if you plant at least three trees, ideally different varieties with bloom times that overlap.

You may want to study and weigh your options, but if you want help with just a simple starter blend, Ashmead's Kernal, Esopus Spitzenberg, Golden Russet, Harry Master's Jersey, Muscadet de Dieppe, and Newton Pippin are classic cider varieties that are available from nurseries. These are all adapted to a wide range of conditions, are relatively disease resistant, and blend into a delicious cider.

While you wait for your own trees to mature, you can start making cider with varieties that you find at nearby pick-your-own orchards and farmers' markets. Gravenstein, a tart heirloom, and Cox's Orange Pippin, an extra-sweet old-fashioned favorite, are enjoying renewed interest from growers. Modern varieties, such as sharp Stayman Winesap and sweet Fuji, can work well together.

You can grow an apple tree from a seed you find inside the fruit, but you will wait many years for it to reach a mature and productive size. But even if it grew faster, you wouldn't want to grow an apple from seed because you'll have no idea what the fruit the tree produces would be like. Apple trees are sold as grafted saplings. That is, the nursery takes fruiting branches from the type of apple you want and fuses them, using a time-tested and safe process, to what's called a rootstock, from another variety. The rootstock (which is often from the closely related quince tree) is chosen because it is thrives in the conditions where it will grow, but if it is left to produce its own fruit you would find that it does not have desirable qualities for eating or making cider. The apple varieties with qualities you want have roots that tend to be too weak or cold sensitive to survive outside of the most protected environments.

A mature apple tree may reach 50 to 60 feet tall. You can choose dwarf versions—the same fruit branches grafted onto rootstocks that naturally peak at about one-third to one-half the size of standard versions. The dwarfs fit comfortably into suburban and small urban lots. If you have even less room, you can find mini varieties that will grow in pots or you might want to check

Columnar Apples

out the columnar apple—a unique type that's all trunk and little branch, so it will fit into a very tight space. A bonus for you: All of the smaller apple trees start bearing fruit at a younger age—typically around three to four years—than the large trees.

SITE

The ideal site for your apple trees gets morning sun and is breezy. Sunshine early in the day and steady air flow dry dew and other moisture from the leaves, flowers, and developing fruit, which helps reduce the risk of fungal diseases forming on them. Well-drained soil—where water doesn't stand for a long time after a rainstorm—is also important. The best spot would be at the top of a slope, because it has maximum sun and air exposure, and moisture drains away from the soil.

PLANTING

Late summer to early fall is the best time to plant an apple tree (and nearly any other type of tree). Spring, after the soil has warmed up past 55°F, is the next best time. If you plant right before a spell of overcast, drizzly weather, the sapling will stay moist as it establishes itself.

Soak the tree's roots in water for an hour before you plant them. When you're ready to plant, dig holes for the saplings that are about twice the size of each root-ball and between 3 and 6 inches deeper. Add a few shovelfuls of compost into the hole and mix it with the soil. Unwrap the tree's root-ball and gently tease out the roots with your fingers. Set the tree in the hole so that the roots and stem are the same level they were in the nursery pot—that is, don't bury it deeper or let the roots stick up above ground. The graft union, which you can see on the trunk, needs to stay aboveground. Once you have the tree set, backfill the hole with the rest of the soil you took out and gently tamp it down so that the roots have good contact with the soil. Moisten but don't drench the soil. Spread mulch, such as pine bark chips or straw (not hay), around the base of the tree to keep the soil consistently damp and to stop weeds from taking root. Don't mound up the mulch like a volcano around the trees' trunks because it can cause rot or give shelter to bark-chewing rodents.

CARE

For the first year, you need to help your apple trees develop by watering them whenever the soil feels dry when you push your index finger in about two knuckles deep. Give them a good soaking so that the water penetrates deep into the soil and encourages the trees' roots to grow down. After the first year, you only need to water the trees during an extended drought (a month or more).

Deep tree roots can also scavenge the soil for the nutrients they require, so you don't need—or want—to pump them up with manufactured fertilizers. Instead, in spring and fall of each year, gently scratch an inch or so of compost into the surface of the soil around the tree's dripline (which is just as it sounds—the area beneath the tree where raindrops will fall from the leaves). The compost provides nutrients the trees need and, just as important, it stimulates the activity of microbes in the soil to help turn organic matter into nourishment for the trees.

Weeds and even grass compete with trees' roots for moisture and nutrients, so you want to keep them away from the trees during the first year or so, until the trees' roots are established. A layer of organic mulch, such as pine bark chips, does this job effectively. Plastic mulch does the job, too, and is easy to use, but it does degrade over time and breaks down into little pieces of plastic that do not nourish the soil as natural materials will. Whatever kind of mulch you use, be sure not to use your lawn mower or string trimmer (a.k.a. weed whacker) so close to the trees' trunks that they are damaged in the process. A damaged tree trunk is an invitation to pests and diseases.

In winter, the sun and cold can combine to damage young trees. On late winter days, the sun can heat up one part of the trunk and the sap inside and prematurely break the dormancy of just that area. When the sun goes down and the temperatures drop to below freezing again, that section of the young trees can be permanently damaged with what's called sunscald. You can protect your trees in their early years with white plastic sleeves. The sleeves also protect them from bark-chewing critters, such as deer and mice. When the trees get to be three or four years old, their bark is thick enough in most cases to withstand sunscald.

Pruning is one of the most important ways to keep your apple trees healthy as they grow and ensures you the best harvest. The best time to prune apple trees is late winter, though you can remove dead or diseased branches whenever you see them.

You can find detailed training diagrams from the cooperative extensions of the universities listed in the Resources section, but the basic principles are simple. Each tree should have a single main trunk and then sturdy lateral branches on opposing sides up the trunk. After the tree's third season, begin to cleanly cut off any branches that cross through the middle of the tree, are growing toward the ground rather than upward, or are overlapping other branches. Cut off any branch that is growing at an angle less than 45 degrees from the trunk. You want the tree to be symmetrical, not for aesthetic reasons; rather, so that air flows freely through the branches. To make sure sunlight can reach fruit on all the branches, trim the top ones a little shorter than the lower branches. When the tree grows to more than 4 feet tall, trim off all the branches lower than 18 inches from the ground.

Serious orchardists train their apples, guiding their growth much the way you do with grapevines (though it's a much slower process because trees take longer than vines to grow). They use weights and other means to control the direction branches grow. This isn't necessary when you're growing only a few trees, because the goal of training the trees is to make mechanized harvesting easier. If you live in a small space, you can espalier apple trees—that is, train them to grow up or against a wall.

Four to six weeks after the trees bloom in spring (and they are beautiful in bloom), they will have lots of little fruit, up to 20 percent of which will drop off. This is a natural and healthy process, ensuring that the tree has enough resources to mature the fruit that remains. You will notice over time that your trees produce more in some years and less in others. That, too, is a natural and healthy process.

Espalier Apple Trees

TROUBLESHOOTING

Apples, like all fruit trees, can be plagued by pests and diseases. The most effective way to keep them healthy and able to resist pests is to give them the conditions they need—lots of morning sun and air circulation. Practice good sanitation—removing all the fallen fruit from beneath your trees reduces the number of pests that make their homes there. Also, if you or other growers nearby have confronted problems in the past, consider planting disease-resistant varieties—there are many to choose from. Planting a mix of varieties also helps minimize problems because one or two of them can be less vulnerable to a particular problem than the others, ensuring that you have at least some apples to harvest.

When you do have problems, do all you can to stick with organic treatments for the problems. Not only are organic methods safer for you and the environment, they don't leave behind residues that will affect the flavor of your cider. Try these simple techniques to control pests and diseases without toxic chemicals.

Apple maggots are small, soft white larvae that tunnel into the fruit after they hatch. Remove the fallen fruit and you greatly decrease the number of apple maggots that spoil your fruit. You can capture the adults before they lay their eggs in your trees with traps made with red balls (about the size and shape of apples) and a sticky substance popularly sold as Tangle-Trap.

Codling moths are grayish brown and emerge when apple trees are in bloom. They lay their eggs on the small, developing fruit and the larvae chew into the core when they hatch. After three to five weeks of feeding, they drop to the ground and pupate into caterpillars, which then climb back into the tree to feed on leaves. Disrupt the caterpillars' return to the tree with sticky tape wrapped around the trunks of the trees. This works best if you control the season's first generation of moths because it drastically reduces the numbers of reproducing moths in the second and possible third generation of the year.

Plum curculio, despite its name, is a beetle that attacks apples, tunneling into the fruit and causing it to rot or drop prematurely. The larvae live and grow in rotting fruit left on the ground, so you can limit their numbers simply by cleaning up beneath your trees. The adults are easy to knock from the trees—just spread a sheet on the ground, lightly tap the tree branches with a stick, and watch the beetles fall. When you've gathered them up, dump them into a bucket of soapy water and they will pester you no more.

Apple scab is a disease that often afflicts apple trees in humid regions. It shows up on flowers and leaves as light gray spots, which darken as they age. Affected fruit will have corky, scablike lesions on their skin. The disease survives from season to season on fallen leaves, so be sure to rake up the leaves in fall when they have been infected. Air circulation is especially helpful for preventing scab, so prune as needed to open the interior branches to a breeze. When the tree is infected with scab, you can use a sulfur spray (available at nurseries and garden centers) as a last resort to control it.

Fire blight comes on fast and leaves a lot of damage in its wake. In late spring, the leaves, flowers, and young shoots wilt and then turn black, looking like they've been burned. It's caused by bacteria that live from year to year on infected twigs until warm spring rains cause it to ooze from cankers on the tree. Insects spread the bacteria to other trees. Minimize the risk by thoroughly pruning any diseased-looking branches (cut about 6 inches below any bark that's cankered or shriveled) every winter. If you discover an infection that's spread beyond one tree, spray all of them with Bordeaux mixture, a blend of copper, sulfur, and lime that's approved for use in organic growing and available at garden centers and online.

HARVESTING

Patience often is the greatest challenge you face when you're growing a crop you want to use. Apples change color before they are fully ripe—their full complement of sugar and flavors develop after the color. And apples don't develop sugars as, for instance, bananas do, and their flavor does not improve after they're picked. Each variety has its own ripening time, and the conditions during the season also affect the ripening time, so you can't just mark your calendar for apple-picking day.

Color, though, is the first indication that the apples are ripening. They all have a ground color, which might be red, yellow, or shades of green. When you buy the trees, the nursery can tell you the ground color of the apple. When the whole apple changes to its ground color, it's begun to ripen. When most of the apples on the tree have changed color, you want to begin tasting them. They should be juicy and crisp, but not hard. The seeds inside should be black, not brown or even lighter.

When you think they are ready, gather three or four from different trees (or parts of one tree) and taste them. Try a couple again a day or two later and repeat for up to a week or two until the flavor of the apples is consistent, which tells you they have reached their peak.

Pick them carefully, discarding any that are moldy or insect infested, but you can keep those with bruises you are able to cut out. If you don't plan to make cider right away, you can store unbruised apples for a couple of weeks in a cool, dry place in baskets or other containers that let air flow around them.

⋉⋉⋉⋉⋉⋉⋉⋉⋉⋉ MAKING CIDER ⋉⋉⋉⋉⋉⋉⋉⋉⋉⋉

The consensus among those who have brewed beer and made wine, mead, and cider is that cider making is the easiest process to manage. Of course, making exceptional cider is just as challenging as making great beer or wine, but the basic process is the simplest. If you haven't yet made fermented drinks, cider is a sensible place to start.

PRESSING

Apple juice is extracted from the fruit by crushing it through a filter. Commercial orchards do this with a large wooden press that screws down and crushes the apples. If you live near a small orchard or old homestead, you may be able to get your apples pressed for a small fee. If not, you can chunk them and blend them in a food processor into a fine, juicy pulp. Pour the pulp into a kitchen sieve over a ceramic bowl and squeeze the juice out by pressing on the pulp with your fist. If you decide you want to make cider regularly, you can buy a tabletop cider press for less than $300. Use a cider-pressing bag or a cheesecloth to be sure that the skins, seeds, stems, and other debris don't get into the juice and leave behind harsh flavors. You can expect to get 4 to 6 gallons of cider for each bushel of apples you press, depending on how juicy the apples are.

Small Cider Press

BUYING JUICE

While you're waiting for your apple trees to begin yielding fruit or whenever you want to complement your own juice with other flavors, sweet cider or concentrated apple juice that has no preservatives other than ascorbic acid can be fermented into hard cider. Pasteurized juices work, but look for those that are cloudy rather than clear—clarified juices are missing the solids that give your hard cider body.

YEAST SELECTION

People first discovered the pleasures of hard cider because indigenous yeasts that will ferment the sugars in the juice occur naturally. Wild yeasts can produce excellent, complex ciders, but they can also yield bitter, yeasty brews with off-flavors. When you use wild yeast, the final alcohol content of the cider is less certain than when you work with cultured yeasts. Because of the unpredictable results, most artisan cider makers rely on cultured yeasts.

If you want to try wild yeasts—and why not try a batch or two so you can taste the difference in the results between wild and cultured?—you can just pour the juice into the primary fermenter, leave off the lid and wait for the bubbling to begin.

Baking yeasts are likely to produce strange-tasting cider. You can find cider-specific yeasts in liquid and powder form from brewing suppliers, but almost any yeast used for making wine or beer will work. Wyeast Ale Yeast is familiar to many home brewers and produces a generally well-balanced cider. Lalvin EC 1118 is dry wine yeast that ferments rapidly and has a comparatively low demand for supplemental nutrients. Red Star Côte des Blancs is a slow-fermenting wine yeast that does require additional nutrients, but produces a smooth, dry cider. Experienced cider makers report that it seems to enhance the cider's natural apple flavor. A single (10-gram) packet of yeast is all you need to make 5 gallons of cider.

MAKING MUST

If you don't plan on relying on wild yeasts, you need to neutralize them before you begin fermenting the juice. Bacteria also live on the skins and pulp of your fruit and may foul your cider if you don't eliminate them. Blending a crushed campden (sulfite) tablet into your juice is the quick and easy way to take out both wild yeasts and bacteria, but it does leave sulfites behind, which cause allergic reactions in some people.

Heating the juice can also accomplish the same goal. Gently simmer the juice in a sterile pot over low to medium heat for about forty-five minutes. Be careful not to let the juice come to a hard boil or its natural pectins will set, making the juice hazy. If you want to make your cider sweeter or more potent, the simmering stage is the best time to add sugar, honey, molasses, concentrated apple juice, or other sweetener. You want to wait until after primary fermentation, however, to add other sorts of flavorings. Use your hydrometer to check to make sure your must is 1.045 to 1.050 specific gravity (SG). Below 1.045 SG, the yeast may not have enough sugar to fully ferment the must. Add sugar (in any of the forms mentioned above) in small amounts, no more than $\frac{1}{4}$

cup at a time, to raise it into this range, if need be. The resulting cider will be about 6 percent alcohol by volume.

When you're done neutralizing the wild yeasts in the juice and getting its sugar content into the recommended range, pour it into your primary fermenter and allow it to cool to room temperature. When the juice is between 60° and 75°F, you can add pectic enzyme, which helps break down pectin, a natural substance that holds cells together and forms clouds in liquid as the alcohol content rises. Pectic enzyme does not affect the flavor. If your blend does not include apples that are rich in tannins—the compounds that give cider and wine their astringency—you can add tannin compounds to the juice before fermentation. Strong black tea is also high in tannins, and you can try using it instead of purchased wine tannins. Blend in yeast nutrients, if you're using a type of yeast that needs a boost for fermenting cider. When using products such as pectic enzyme, wine tannin blends, and yeast nutrients, follow the package instructions carefully to avoid leaving behind residues that will alter the flavor of your cider. If you choose strong black tea as a source of tannins, add about $1/2$ cup per gallon of must.

After all the ingredients are blended in, pitch your yeast and stir it in thoroughly. Close the lid and place the fermenter where the temperatures stay consistently between 60° to 75°F (the cooler end of the range is better than the high end). When colder, the cider may stop fermenting, and at higher temperatures fermentation speeds up but keeps the flavor from developing fully.

FERMENTING FULLY

In a day or so, bubbles begin to form in the juice, signaling that carbon dioxide is forming and fermentation has commenced. If you have seen no or very few bubbles after forty-eight hours, your yeast may be expired and you need to pitch again with fresh yeast. The vigorous bubbling stops in about two weeks and the primary fermentation is over. You now have a yeasty, sweet lightly alcoholic drink. If you wait a week or so, some of the yeastiness will dissipate and you can begin to enjoy it or bottle it to drink later. At this stage, your cider will be cloudy and "still," or uncarbonated.

Racking the cider into a second container and letting it ferment for another four to six weeks allows it to clarify and enhances the cider's taste. The sediment in the bottom of the jug is mostly pulp from the fruit and bitter-tasting dead yeast. Check with a hydrometer and when the reading is 1.005 SG, the cider is ready to be racked. When racking, leave behind an inch or two of cider above the sediment, so that you don't suck any into the tube.

You can choose at this point to add flavorings, such as vanilla, ginger, or crab apple juice, to your cider. Use these flavors sparingly, as their tastes will be magnified during the longer, secondary fermentation, and you don't want them to overwhelm the cider's. Be sure you mix them thoroughly into the must.

Remember to put the airlock on your carboy or other secondary fermenter and keep the container in a cool, dark place. Check it after six weeks and if it is clear and you like the flavor, you can bottle it and drink it whenever you want. As with wine, the flavor does mature and typically improves with age. Three days before you rack or bottle your cider, move the container to the spot—on a shelf or stand—where you will work with it. Moving the container stirs up sediment, which you want to settle again before you siphon out the contents.

Cider will mellow over time (like wine) and the taste will become smoother with less harsh notes. If you are patient, you can let your cider rest in that secondary jug for one to two months, or even give it a third rack and let it hang out for four to six months. (Leaving it in secondary too long can make it taste yeasty—so rack it into a clean jug if you are going to age more than eight weeks.) Time allows the processes of malolactic fermentation to kick in, and breaks down the harsher "vinegary" taste sometimes found in young brew. But young brew is tasty, too, so it is your call. If this is your third batch, or you are experimenting with multiple jugs, do set one aside to age for a bit and see the difference.

You can make bubbly sparkling cider by adding sweet syrup to your cider just before you bottle it. Make the syrup by boiling $^3/_4$ cup of honey or sugar in a cup of water. Thoroughly blend it with 5 gallons must, then bottle it. The remaining yeast will ferment the added sugar in about two months, releasing carbon dioxide, which creates the carbonation bubbles inside the bottle or container. It takes a minimum of two weeks for the carbonation to occur, so wait at least that long before you drink it.

The best bottles for carbonated cider are resealable (swing-top style) bottles like some European beers are sold in; capped beer bottles (not twist-offs!) also work. Champagne bottles are a great option, but you need a specific tool to get the cork into the bottle firmly. Cider continues to ferment in the bottle and increase in carbonation, so you need bottles that can withstand pressure. If your cider is still, you can use any sterile glass container—even mason jars. Just as with wine, aging your cider in oak or other wooden barrels for months or even a year adds the breadth and depth of flavors that the experts get.

×××××××××××× VARIATIONS ××××××××××××

Like apples, pears have a long history as the main ingredient in cider, especially in the United Kingdom, where the resulting drink is known as perry. Pears also can be rich in tannins, acids and a complex of flavors, but again, like apples, the varieties you most commonly find in supermarkets are sweet dessert types rather than those best suited to making cider. To get those pears, you need to find an orchard specializing in heirloom varieties or grow your own.

VARIETALS. Pears are classified as sweet, medium sharp (more acid, low tannins), bittersweet (low acid, high tannins), and bittersharp (high acid, high tannins). Those bittersharp types are nearly unpalatable eaten fresh, but they make the best perry. Most of the varieties that fall into that category are old-fashioned types found in a few counties in England, but you can find a few modern options at nurseries. Tayton Squash and Blakeney Red are a couple of varieties sold in the United States.

Pear trees are grafted like apples, but usually on pear rootstock, which is hardy enough to survive winter in all but the coldest zones of North America. You can get semidwarf pear trees, which top out at 30 to 40 feet tall, but dwarf cider pear trees are rare. Pear trees of any size take longer to mature and start bearing fruit later than apples, which is why orchardists often say that you plant pears for your heirs.

PLANTING, CARE, AND MAINTENANCE. Pear trees need the same conditions as apple trees—though they can tolerate heavier, damper soil than their cousins—and require the same care. Pears are easy to train and even espalier, and they live and bear fruit for decades, so choose a site where they can be left for a long time.

HARVESTING. Pears differ from apples at ripening time. Whereas apples reach their peak of sweetness on the tree, pears continue ripening after they fall or are picked from the tree. Traditional perry makers wait until the fruit falls before gathering them.

Store the pears for up to a week in a cool, dry place away from sunlight. Press on the flesh; when it softens, they're ripe. With a refractometer, you can test the sugar content of a small sample—just as with grapes, it's the most reliable way to know that the fruit has reached its peak.

MAKING PERRY. The process of making cider with pears is no different than making it with apples. Because even the most acidic pears are sweeter than apples, you don't need to add sugar to the juice. And even commercial perry producers in Europe rely on indigenous yeasts to ferment pears.

I realize I've told you that you'll have to wait some time before your pears ripen and that cider varieties are limited in the United States, so you may not find them at your local farmers' market. Does this mean you have to give up on making perry and regret the time you've spent reading this section? I hope not—on either count. You can blend the juice of sweet pear varieties—Bosc is a good choice—with that from more acidic apples and/or crab apples.

CRAB APPLES

The crab apple tree will prove the accuracy of its name when you bite into its hard, red little fruits—they are highly astringent and too bitter to eat raw. But wth its high tannic acid content, crab apple juice is an ideal addition to cider made with sweet apples or pears.

The crab apple is the fastest way to get started making cider with ingredients you harvest. Apple trees are not native to North America, but four varieties of crab apple are. You'll see them growing wild in every region but the hottest and driest. Crab apples bred for dramatic ruffly pink flowers in spring are used as landscape trees in corporate parks and residential neighborhoods. You can often forage the fruit from trees planted in public places, without much fight from anyone but the birds and squirrels that rely on it for food.

Crab apple trees are worth planting in nearly every yard. The trees stay small—typically less than 20 feet tall—and begin producing fruit in five years or less (after you plant a sapling). They produce a great volume of fruit and it stays on the tree for weeks on end, giving you and wildlife time to gather all that you want. (The blossoms attract both bees and hummingbirds.) If you have or will be planting apple trees, crab apples work as a universal pollinator for apples.

CIDER: THE BACKSTORY

THERE'S NO YOUTUBE VIDEO OR EVEN STONE TABLETS TO PROVE IT, BUT CHANCES are the earliest humans to store food found that apple juice ferments and that once fermented it was safe and pleasurable to drink. By the time of the Roman Empire, many of the tribes of northern Europe were already drinking a fermented apple beverage. The Romans brought apple cultivation to France and England, and by the Middle Ages, cider making was part of every farmer's routine and an art in the hands of monks and others.

The tree botanists call *Malus domestica* originated in western Asia and had spread throughout Europe, but it did not grow in North America, though several related species of crab apples did. The colonists who first settled in Virginia and Massachusetts brought apple tree seedlings with them and found that they flourished in both climates.

By colonial times, cider making had become a commercial enterprise as well as an easy way for farmers to preserve apples and keep a safe supply of fluids to drink. Even the founding fathers extolled the virtues of cider. Thomas Jefferson wrote in his garden journals and letters about the champagnelike cider he created from the Virginia Hewe's Crab apple. John Adams reportedly drank a tankard of cider before breakfast every day to settle his stomach. In the presidential election of 1840, Whig candidate William Henry Harrison appealed to ordinary voters with the symbols of "log cabin and hard cider."

Remember the heartwarming story that we all learned in elementary school about Johnny Appleseed, the good citizen who brought healthy fruit to all the boys and girls? In truth, John Chapman (who became known as "Johnny Appleseed") did start nurseries and orchards as he traveled through nineteenth-century America. The purpose of those orchards was to produce apples to make a fermented cider. Preserving apple juice to drink was more than an indulgence to rural Americans. In a time before municipal sewage treatment, cider was often safer to drink than water. Fermenting was the most reliable and even safest way to preserve apple juice when there was no refrigeration.

Cider remained America's most popular drink even after the water supply became more trustworthy. Prohibition brought a ban on the production and sale of hard cider, just as it did other types of alcohol. In its wake, the emergence of organized criminal—and later commercial—interests supporting beer and hard spirits distribution and the expansion of domestic wine production left cider to a dwindling number of enthusiasts who brewed it for themselves, family, and friends.

People in the United Kingdom, France, Sweden, and other European countries have continued to craft and enjoy fine ciders and perrys, and the back-road cidery has long been a celebrated stop for bicycle tourists in those countries. In the late 1990s, commercial brewers, such as Boston Beer Co. (Samuel Adams brands), began introducing cider varieties to customers in North America with the hope of capturing the market of people who prefer their drinks sweeter than suds. Woodchuck, an independent, Vermont-based producer, now has nearly 50 percent of commercial cider sales in the United States. These commercial hard ciders usually are made with apple juice concentrate, contain about 5 percent alcohol, and are carbonated and overwhelmingly sweet.

The local food movement that has brought heirloom tomatoes and apples to back into circulation and the success of microbreweries in recent years has stimulated renewed interest in handcrafted, unique ciders blended and aged by artisans in small batches. These ciders are now served like wine in restaurants and available for sale both directly from the producer and in other retail outlets. You will meet one of the new breed of cider artisans in the profile below.

SPOTLIGHT ON: FOGGY RIDGE CIDER, DUGSPUR, VIRGINIA

DIANE FLYNT'S VERY SUCCESSFUL AND REWARDING CAREER IN BANKING AND finance took her far from her small-town roots, but the native of Georgia never forgot the quiet pleasures of rural life. "My grandfather was a farmer," she says, "and I always kept such happy memories of the times I spent on his land."

In the 1990s, Flynt and her husband, Chuck, had achieved their corporate career goals, but wanted a different life. They began looking for land on which they could live and work. "We wanted a true rural property and to grow and make a value-added agricultural product—we weren't looking just for a country estate to retire on."

As they visited properties in the hills of Virginia and North Carolina, they saw a lot of land with apple orchards, and discovered how well-suited the climate was for growing heirloom apple varieties. They settled in Virginia's Albermarle County, in the Blue Ridge Mountains, not far from Charlottesville and Monticello, where Thomas Jefferson enjoyed success growing a wide variety of crops, including an array of apples for making cider. In the meantime, Flynt visited and worked in cideries in Europe, learning the craft.

Today, Flynt has her hands on every aspect of producing cider, from pruning the trees to bottling her award-winning blends, served in restaurants and sold in retail outlets in the region. She has carefully chosen varieties suited to her conditions and the flavors she's aiming for. Her selections include the well-known American heirlooms, Cox's Orange Pippin and Roxbury Russet, the Virginia Hewe's Crab grown by presidents Washington and Jefferson, and high-tannin European varieties such as Dabinett and Muscadett de Berney.

"Great cider is a three-legged stool that strikes a balance of sweetness, acidity, and astringency," Flynt says. "Every year, the crop is different and every batch of cider is different. The weather conditions, the age of the trees, when you pick the apples . . . all affect the flavor. The art and craft of cider making is in the adjustments you make in the process."

If you have an interest in following her footsteps, Flynt advises that you do an apprenticeship with an experienced cider producer, so you understand not only the process of making it on a larger scale and the business, about which she is hopeful but realistic, with much of the market dominated by mass-produced brands. She now offers three different ciders—First Fruit, Sweet Stayman, and Serious Cider—and a blend of cider and apple brandy she calls Pippin Gold.

CHAPTER 5

A HONEY OF A DRINK

YOU PROBABLY DON'T WANT TO THINK ABOUT IT QUITE THAT WAY, but bee vomit is one of Nature's most extraordinary substances. Honey, a much more appealing name than "bee puke," is more than just spoil-proof food for queen bees and their children. It is a natural preservative for human food, an antibacterial dressing for wounds, and an anti-inflammatory when consumed. It is a tasty, whole-food sweetener with a unique, authentic flavor all its own. And it is an easy-to-ferment raw ingredient that you can harvest yourself, no matter where you live.

Mead is simply honey wine. It was almost certainly discovered accidentally by the earliest people in Africa, but anthropologists believe that has been produced intentionally for two thousand years or more. Mead making reached its peak in the early medieval period in Europe, but was later supplanted by grape wine as it became more available to ordinary people. Today, mead is enjoying a revival in North America among home fermenters and artisans crafting and bottling their own unique blends.

✕✕✕✕✕✕✕✕✕✕✕ KEEPING BEES ✕✕✕✕✕✕✕✕✕✕✕

Maintaining a colony of bees may seem like a serious, time-consuming effort suitable for large farms far from population centers, but beekeeping has become popular among people who dwell in urban and suburban areas because it is fun, easy-to-do, and entertaining. In a small space—about the size of a filing cabinet—you can keep an active hive that will yield 50 pounds or more each year of fresh and tasty honey that you can use to make your own mead. At the same time, the hardworking insects will do the important work of pollinating many of the vegetables and fruits in your gardens and others nearby. Bees will also entertain you with their diligent building, feeding, and caring for their queen.

Bees do frighten many people, I realize, but unless you or someone in your family has had a powerful allergic reaction to bee stings, you needn't be afraid to keep bees. Unlike wasps, such as the all-too-familiar, bee-resembling yellow jacket, bees typically die when their barbed stinger catches in your skin (it's ripped out of the bees' abdomen, in case you're wondering). So bees avoid the death penalty of stinging except in moments of desperation, such as

when their queen is threatened. If you leave them alone, they'll keep clear of you—though they may be attracted to the floral fragrances used in soaps, perfumes, and other products. Try not to use them when working with or around bees.

BEST BREEDS

Of the thousands of species of bees, only a few of them produce harvestable honey or even live in a hive. Many wild bees nest, feed, and care for their larvae in small groups or even alone. Honeybees are not native to North America—they were brought here by the earliest European colonists—but they have been domesticated for centuries and have been bred into one of four strains. The strains are Italian (a.k.a. Western), Caucasian (from the mountains of Eastern Europe), Black, and Grey (or Carniolan). The Italian and Grey types thrive in man-made hives. If you live in a densely populated area, the Greys are a good choice because they are gentle and have strong homing instincts. They don't fare well in very hot climates, so if you live in the Southeast or Southwest, you're better off with the Italian strain.

HIVE CHOICES

A honeybee hive is an amazingly precise structure built by thousands of insects working together for their common good. The hive comprises a series of panels formed by adjoining evenly sized, six-sided "cells." The bees make the honeycomb from beeswax, and they fill the cells with their queen's children (larvae) and honey on which she and the children feed, and that make for delicious mead. Bees devote much of their time and energy in the first year of a hive to building honeycomb and less to making honey.

Langstroth hives are the most widely used structure for keeping bees and you'd probably recognize them. They look like a set of stacked boxes, though they're really a set of eight to ten wooden or plastic frames in which the bees build their honeycomb. The hive sits on a wire foundation and can be covered easily in foul weather. Beekeepers remove the frames as they fill with honey and can extract the honey without damaging the comb, so the bees can keep making fresh honey without rebuilding the comb. If you're just starting out with beekeeping, the Langstroth design is your best bet because you will find the most information and support from the many others who are using the box hives.

Top-bar hives, which have honeycomb frames placed horizontally and no foundation, have become popular with beekeepers in recent years because they are closer to how bees build when they construct their hives naturally. Top-bar hives are also relatively easy to build with salvaged materials. However, the top-bar setup tends to yield less honey and when you harvest it the comb is often damaged and chunks of it can get into the honey.

The classic wicker bee skep is attractive in an old-fashioned sort of way. Skeps are made from woven straw and are open on the bottom—you must set

Langstroth Hive

them on grass or other natural surface, so they're not a good choice if you are keeping bees on a balcony or rooftop.

No matter which sort of hive you choose to keep, you want to mimic bees' natural instincts when choosing a location for it. Bees build hives where they're sheltered from heavy winds and precipitation, so you should set it close to a wall, fence, or hedgerow to protect it from the wind and harsh weather. A partially shaded location is the bees' preference. Set the hive as high as you can reach and the bees coming and going from the hive will mostly fly over the heads of your neighbors. Speaking of which, do all you can to place your hive where it won't be seen by passersby—at the least, set the hives 25 feet or more from sidewalks and roads, so the daily activity around the hive doesn't attract attention from and is not troubled by passersby.

Early spring is the best time to start a beehive. You can order bees from a mail-order source, which will send you a package with a queen and several thousand workers. You may be able to get a colony from a swarm catcher in your area, but I suggest you start with a beginner's kit, if you've never kept bees before. Be sure to have your hive and all your supplies ready to go before you order. When the bees do arrive, late afternoon on an overcast day is the best time to introduce them to your new hive.

CARE AND MAINTENANCE

Bees feed primarily on flower nectar and the honey they make from it. If you have room to plant a diverse garden full of flowers, herbs, vegetables, and fruits, your bees will have a steady nectar supply. Their favorite flowers are borage (a.k.a. bee's bread), lilacs, monarda (a.k.a. bee balm), and goldenrod. In the early spring and late fall, when natural food may be scarce for your bees, you can supplement their diet with syrup (sugar and water solution). Bees also need water nearby. During dry spells, a simple birdbath or shallow dish of water will be enough for them.

The queen, her workers (females who provide food for the queen and the brood, and care for the hive), and the drones (males whose only purpose is reproduction) have evolved specific roles that help the hive sustain itself. Your role, then, is to stay out of the way and help only when problems occur. By providing the bees with the conditions that they need, you minimize the potential problems. One common mistake that many new beekeepers make is setting up a hive that is too big for the size of the colony. The extra space leaves room that the bees can't police themselves, creating an opportunity for pests that prey on bees to move in.

Wax moths, beetles, mites, and viruses sometimes invade honeybee hives, and there are a variety of chemical treatments available for dealing with them. Many small-scale beekeepers, though, are able to do without the pesticides and antibiotics, relying instead on the bees' natural defenses to overcome problems. For instance, wax moths often get into a hive (attracted by the wax, hence their name) and lay eggs. When the larvae (little grubs) hatch, they eat honeycomb and honey, spin webbing into a cocoon and turn into moths. In a healthy colony, the bees kill the grubs before they do much damage.

✕✕✕✕✕✕✕✕✕✕✕✕✕ A FRIEND OF BEES ✕✕✕✕✕✕✕✕✕✕✕✕✕

HONEYBEES, ESPECIALLY THOSE KEPT IN COMMERCIAL-SCALE OPERATIONS, began in the 2000s to suffer from a mysterious epidemic scientists dubbed colony collapse disorder. It continues to threaten not only the livelihood of professional beekeepers and many farmers, but also the supply of many foods. Researchers have advanced different theories on the cause of colony collapse disorder, in which hives are found completely abandoned and no bees left behind to study. While they figure it out, you can do three important things to help bees, whether you are tending hives or not.

1. Don't use pesticides! The chemicals used to kill bugs of any kind may be toxic to honey bees.

2. Avoid GMOs. Genetically modified crops have pesticides spliced into their DNA. The risk to honey bees of GMOs has never been studied, but many environmentalists are concerned that bees collecting pollen from these plants could be carrying the pesticide back to their hives. You can help protect them by buying organic food, which by law cannot contain GMOs, or genetically modified organisms.

3. Plant nectar. In the creeping monoculture that is most inhabited areas of the United States, bees have fewer and fewer choices for feeding. Do them—and yourself—a favor and plant a wide variety of flowers and herbs around your home. Be sure to include monarda (bee balm), one of their favorites.

HONEY HARVEST

If you are keeping bees to harvest their honey, you want to have a protective suit that looks sort of like a cross between the protective gear you wear when handling hazardous materials and the outfits worn by spacemen in comic books. You also want a bee smoker, which is a small vessel in which you burn bark, pine needles, dried grass, or sage and then puff into the hive with the smoker's bellows *(fig. A)*.

Smoke causes the bees to become more docile, so you can open the hive while they are sedated. The best times to go into a hive are during the midday hours in early to midsummer, when the workers are out in the field collecting nectar.

Each of the frames in the hive's super contains honey, so you'll remove each frame and brush off the bees (gently!) with a soft brush before harvesting the honey *(fig. B)*. Use a capping scratcher to remove the wax layer from each cell, then load the frames in the extractor *(fig. C)*. An extractor is specially designed to separate honey from the comb and is the most efficient way to harvest it while least damaging to the hive. You can often borrow an extractor from other beekeepers or apiary groups in your area. If you can't, you can crush the comb with the honey in a bucket that has a screen to catch the comb and a spigot at the bottom called a honey gate, from which it drips out *(fig. D)*.

figure A

figure B

figure C

figure D

✕✕✕✕✕✕✕✕✕✕✕✕✕ HONEY CURES ✕✕✕✕✕✕✕✕✕✕✕✕✕✕✕

WHETHER YOU HARVEST YOUR OWN HONEY OR BUY IT FROM A LOCAL BEEKEEPER, it is a valuable local resource. Here are a few fascinating facts about it.

• Honey stays fresh at room temperature. No need to refrigerate it.

• Cookies, cakes, and other baked goods made with honey stay fresher longer because honey absorbs and retains moisture.

• Honey has natural antiseptic properties and has been used for centuries to coat open wounds and protect them from infection.

• Your grandmother was right: Tea with honey soothes a sore throat. That's because honey reduces inflammation.

✕✕✕✕✕✕✕✕✕ SPOTLIGHT ON: MERRY MEADERY ✕✕✕✕✕✕✕✕✕

BRAD DAHLHOFER AND HIS FRIEND PAUL ZIMMERMAN HAD BEEN AMATEUR HOME brewers of beer, cider, mead, and wine since the 1990s. By 2005, they were producing meads that were good enough to win medals at local competitions, and in 2008, they, along with Brad's wife, Kerri, turned their hobby into a thriving new business, B. Nektar Meadery in Ferndale, Michigan. Today, they produce a dozen different varieties of mead, ranging from simple dry Orange Blossom to Backwoods Cyser (made with unpasteurized local apple cider) to Bourbon Barrel Mead, which has a 17.5 percent ABV and a hint of bourbon flavor.

"Making mead is simpler than brewing beer because you are dealing with just a few ingredients and a very basic process," Zimmerman says. "But to make great mead is challenge because you need to start with the best ingredients and you have to pay careful attention to every step in the process."

The partners built relationships with local beekeepers and farmers to source their ingredients. In 2012, they signed on a beekeeper to tend their own hives. They've also studied with the legendary mead maker Ken Schramm to refine their process. He partnered with them on a series of signature meads they began releasing in the summer of 2011. The Heart of Darkness mead was made from Schramm's own morello cherries, black currants, and red raspberries.

"Any decent sweet mead has a nice flavor, but the really superior ones have a very smooth finish with no hints of sulfur and an alcohol content that doesn't overwhelm the flavor of the honey and other ingredients," Zimmerman explains. "Getting those balances right is a learning process. The good news is, even your mistakes can taste pretty good." To learn more and see all of their products, go to www.bnektar.com.

✕✕✕✕✕✕✕✕✕✕✕✕ MAKING MEAD ✕✕✕✕✕✕✕✕✕✕✕✕

Basic mead is a simple drink made with essentially two ingredients, honey and water. Of course, that means your results depend solely on the quality of those ingredients and the care you take in the fermentation process. Even if you add other flavors to make melomel or other variations on mead (learn more about them on page 150), you cannot hide or compensate for poor-quality honey or water with off-flavors.

If you keep bees and harvest the honey, you will know about its quality and purity, and many if not all of the nectar sources that the bees visited. Provide for them a wide variety of flowering plants and you will ensure that the honey's flavor is rich and well balanced.

If you aren't keeping your own hives or they don't yet produce all the honey that you want, look for a local beekeeper who sells it (see Resources to find one near you). Farmers' markets today often include local honey producers. The honey typically sold by national brands in supermarkets has been filtered and heated to a high temperature, killing off the beneficial enzymes it naturally contains and leaving the taste just blandly sweet. In some cases, mass-produced, generic honey for grocery stores has been blended with corn syrup to keep it clear, stabilize the viscosity, and extend the shelf life. You want to steer clear of those products—they won't ferment properly.

Raw honey has never been heated or filtered—just extracted from the comb and bottled. Over time, raw honey gradually crystallizes, turning from a thick liquid to almost solid. With some types of honey that can happen in a month; with others, the crystallization takes many months and maybe even years. Many suppliers treat their honey at a lower temperature (below 120°F) to help slow crystallization.

When buying honey you will see such varietals as clover honey or orange blossom honey, the two most widely sold types. These designations indicate the primary nectar sources for the bees, and that does have a distinct affect on the honey's flavor. Both of those have become popular for their mild flavor and bright color. Goldenrod honey makes the best mead, many brewers believe, and it can help allergy sufferers inoculate themselves from the weed's pollen. Buckwheat honey is darker, maltier, and maybe more nutritious, but it's not easy to make into tasty mead.

Using locally sourced honey not only supports the beekeepers in your community and ensures that you get a minimally processed product, it will help you learn what your honey should taste like. Orange blossom honey, for instance, can only be locally produced if you live in regions where citrus fruits grow, meaning primarily Florida, the Gulf Coast, and Southern California. Your own honey will carry the flavors of the plants that grow where you are. As you begin to develop your experience making mead, you want to taste as many different kinds of honey as possible, both before and after you ferment it. Veteran mead makers, like vintners, develop a strong sense of how the mead will turn out just by sampling the honey beforehand. When starting out, you want to be sure to avoid honey that has a musty or very acidic aroma.

YEAST OPTIONS

You can now find yeasts specifically packaged for making mead, but you can use cider, beer, and wine yeasts, too. The yeasts that make dry or sweet wine will have the same effect on mead. Wine varieties are more alcohol tolerant, so they will survive and continue feeding on the honey's abundant sugar longer than beer or cider types. If you want to try a beer yeast, go with one of those that produce ale, such as Wyeast 1056, because they have a higher alcohol tolerance than other types.

For your first batches, you might want to stick with proven reliable choices, such as Narbonne (Lalvin 71b-1122) or Tokay for sweet meads. For a drier taste, consider a white wine or champagne yeast, such as Rudisheimer or Premier Cuvée. Once you've successfully made a batch or two, you'll want to experiment with different yeasts, because each affects the flavor, alcohol content, clarity, and speed of fermentation.

Liquid yeasts work best in mead if you start them in a weak honey and water solution a day or two day before pitching, which dramatically increases their population and puts them in a kind of feeding frenzy right when you want them to get busy in your must. If you choose less expensive dry yeasts (which offer you more choices), you can rehydrate them just before you pitch them. In a sanitized dish or measuring cup, stir it into warm (90°F) water according to the package directions and stir thoroughly to be sure it has all dissolved. Do this just a few minutes before your must is ready for it. A single packet (10 grams) of yeast is typically enough for each 5-gallon batch of mead.

PREPARE THE MUST

Blending the honey and water to get it ready to ferment takes just a few steps. First, the honey is pasteurized in hot water to kill bacteria, wild yeasts, and other microbes that will compete with the yeast and create off-flavors in your mead. Then you bring down the temperature rapidly with cool water, so that it's not too hot for the yeast. Some experienced mead makers skip the heating step, but when you're a beginner it's worth, I think, taking the extra precautions to increase your chances of success.

Experts debate whether to boil the honey before fermenting. Boiling advocates prefer to vaporize any impurities in the honey, such as beeswax residue, and create a more stable must. If you decide to boil the honey, leave it on for about ten minutes and use a strainer to skim off the foam that forms on top. Antiboilers believe the high heat also vaporizes subtle flavor compounds and kills off vital, desirable enzymes in the honey. They pasteurize, or kill wild yeast and bacteria, by heating the honey to 165°F for 20 minutes. Whichever method you choose, you need to add some water to the honey before heating, and then blend it with the remainder of your water after the heating process is done.

The antiboilers are persuasive, so here I will explain their method. To make 5 gallons of mead, start with about 5 quarts (or 12 to 15 pounds) of honey and 4 gallons of water. Put 3 gallons of the water in your refrigerator and pour the other gallon into a sterilized stockpot. Bring the water to a full boil, then turn off the heat. Pour the honey into the stockpot—you can use a little of the hot water to loosen any honey that stays stuck in the jar. Add the yeast nutrient and stir the mixture well until the honey and water are completely blended.

Check the temperature of the honey blend—you want it above 150°F, but no hotter than 165°F. Put on the lid and let it sit for about fifteen minutes. While you wait, pour the 3 gallons of chilled water into your fermentation bucket. After the fifteen-minute waiting period, mix the honey blend with the cool water in the bucket. The temperature now should be a lot closer to 80°F. When it cools to that level, pitch your yeast. Then stir. With vigor. For as long as you can—up to five minutes. You're giving the yeast air that will fuel its growth, and the faster and more exuberantly it grows, the more it will consume the honey's sugar and convert it to alcohol.

Move the bucket to a spot where it's out of the way for the next two weeks, but where you can still check on it. Seal the lid. Watch for the bubbling to begin in about twenty-four hours. Check on it daily. After about two weeks you'll see that the bubbling has slowed down to occasionally.

When the rapid bubbling has finished, set the bucket on a stool or shelf and let it settle for twenty-four hours. Rack the mead into a sanitized carboy, put the airlock on it, and set it in a spot where it will be out of the way for two months. You can taste your mead at that time, but don't be surprised if it tastes too sweet at that point. Mead's flavor mellows with aging.

You can use beer or wine bottles to age your mead, whichever you are set up for. Aging in oak barrels adds depth to the flavor, just as it does for wine. You can get some of the same benefits by using oak chips, which are available from winemaking suppliers. You can also age it in a sanitized, repurposed beer or soda keg, under CO_2 pressure. Be patient: Aging makes dramatic differences in mead. Wait a year or more to drink your mead and you'll be rewarded with a flavor that's smoother and more nuanced. Mead's flavors are best showcased when it's at room temperature, though you can drink it chilled, if you like.

⨯⨯⨯⨯⨯⨯⨯⨯⨯⨯⨯⨯ VARIATIONS ON MEAD ⨯⨯⨯⨯⨯⨯⨯⨯⨯⨯⨯⨯

FROM THE SIMPLEST OF INGREDIENTS COMES A VAST OCEAN OF POSSIBILITIES. IN its long history, mead has been introduced to the world's many flavorings. Along the way, it gathered a unique set of terms to describe the variations.

SHOW MEAD: just two ingredients and no carbonation

SACK MEAD: extra honey makes it sweeter and stronger

MELOMEL: flavored with fruit; also known as mulsum

METHEGLIN: spiced mead

PYMENT: blended with grape juice

BRAGGOT: malt and hops added

CYSER: cider and mead together

MORAT: with mulberries

ADDING SPARKLE

To turn still, or uncarbonated, mead into a bubbly, sparkling drink, you initiate a second fermentation just before bottling it. The carbon dioxide that the yeast emits produces the bubbles (during the first fermentation you let them out through your airlock). The second fermentation also increases the mead's alcohol content.

After racking the mead off the sediment, add sugar—3/4 to 1 cup to 5 gallons—to the must. After waiting twelve to twenty-four hours to reactivate the yeast, bottle the mead, and seal the bottles with lids.

These bottles are now under serious pressure. To keep them from exploding, be sure to leave $\frac{1}{4}$ inch of headspace in each bottle and make sure the seal is complete and tight.

FLAVOR CHANGERS

The basic formula of honey and water with no carbonation produces what is known as show mead, or traditional mead. You can make it sweeter and stronger (14 percent or more ABV content) by adding more honey to create sack mead. Once you've made and enjoyed a few batches of these basic meads, you may be ready to begin adding homegrown ingredients, such as fruit, flowers, herbs, and spices that impart their own natural flavors to your mead. These variations have unique names (see the list on page 150) and let you create meads to pair with almost any meal and taste.

Fruit of all kinds add flavor, fragrance, and color to melomel, as fruit-flavored mead is called. You can make melomel with juice concentrates and other shortcuts, but using your homegrown whole fruit is so easy and it truly is a very satisfying way to preserve some of the most perishable foods from your garden.

While fruit is sweet, it also brings with it other flavor components that can balance the high sugar component of the honey. Berries and citrus fruits add an acidic note to the melomel. Your choices include strawberries, raspberries, blueberries, blackberries, currants, and mulberries. Grapes, apples, and pears—particularly the high-tannin varieties prized for cider-making—and pie cherries impart astringency to the mead, giving a final taste that's drier and less sugary. Summer fruits, such as peaches, plums, and melons, highlight the floral aroma and flavors in the honey. (For information on

growing, harvesting, and preparing all of these fruits,
check the winemaking chapter, or the cider chapter, in the
case of apples and pears.)

The safest time to add fruit to your mead is after the primary fermentation is over and
you rack it for the first time. The alcohol content of the mead will neutralize any wild
yeasts or bacteria that are on the fruit, and the yeast you're using will have spent itself on
the honey so it won't aggressively ferment the fruit sugars before the flavor has been
passed on to the mead. You can put the fruit in your carboy and rack the mead on top of it.
You then have to filter out the fruit when you next rack it, about two months later. If your
setup allows, you can float the fruit in the mead in a muslin bag or cheesecloth to reduce
the amount of particulate that the fruit leaves behind in your mead.

Grapes, apples, or pears work best if they are first pressed—with the skins on but the
stems removed—just as you would for making a wine or cider with them. The skins
contain much of the tannins that produce the astringent flavor contrast to the honey's
sweetness. To flavor with cherries, add a small amount of tart cherry juice to your must,
or slice and add them after primary fermentation and you've racked the mead once.
Slice peaches, plums, and melons, and remove the pits or seeds, but leave the skins (for
peaches and plums) on the flesh. You can add berries whole. Add fruit to your must
after the primary fermentation is over and you've racked the mead once.

The amount of fruit to use depends on how strong you want the fruit flavor to be.
Start with 3 to 5 pounds of a fruit for your first 5-gallon batch of melomel, to see how it
affects the flavor. If you'd like an even fruitier drink, one that is close to fruit wine, you
can use 10 or more pounds of fruit in 5 gallons of mead.

In mead's glory days—from the medieval period through the Age of Enlighten-
ment—it was the preferred drink of the nobility (for more on that, see "Mead: The Back-
story" on page 155) and herbs and spices were an expected ingredient. Those potent
flavorings, mostly imported from Asia, were highly valued in those times and including them in mead was an expression of affluence. They also added a spark of unique
flavor to the basic mead taste, and today's mead makers continue to use them in creating their own concoctions. Spiced mead is particularly popular as a mulled, or warmed,
drink served during the winter holidays. Chefs and home cooks also use spiced mead
as a marinade or cooking sauce. Mead made with herbs and spices is called metheglin.
You can buy extracts of herbs and spices, known as gruit, instead of using fresh, homegrown flavorings.

A wide variety of spices blend well into mead. Ginger, cinnamon, cloves, and nutmeg are the most common choices, but allspice, cardamom, and vanilla also have been used in award-winning meads. Saffron is expensive and its flavor can overpower the honey's, but used judiciously it gives the mead a rich, appealing golden hue.

Herbs are less potent than spices, yet still impart their unique flavors to mead. And most herbs you can grow yourself (as you can see on page 180). Among the best herbs you can grow for flavoring mead are anise, basil, bergamot (not the citrus fruit, but a kind of monarda), chamomile, coriander (actually, the seeds from the cilantro plant), fennel, lavender, lemon balm, mint, roses (petals and hips), and sweet woodruff. Each changes the character of the mead, so use them individually before you try blends, which can easily go awry.

Chile peppers, from the mild jalapeño to the fiery habanero, are classified scientifically as a fruit, but their flavor functions more like a spice in your mead. Their heat provides a distinctive contrast to the sweet honey, but tread lightly—you don't want your drink to burn on the way down. Try adding one small pepper to 5 gallons of mead after primary fermentation and you've racked it once.

Juniper berries give gin its crisp, acidic taste and those same qualities can complement the sweetness of mead. They're not actually berries—they're the dried seed cones from the evergreen shrub/small tree. To release their many volatile oils—the source of their flavor and fragrance—you need to crush them a little between your fingers. Drop a few of the crushed cones into the must after it's fermented.

Whichever spices and herbs you choose to try, use just a small amount in your first batch or two because their flavors can be so strong. You also want to add them to the drink after the primary fermentation is over and you've racked it once. You can try adding the spices to the original must, but they can disrupt or sidetrack the yeasts' process. It's better to put them in a spice or tea ball (or in a muslin bag) and drop it into the mead after racking it. Taste your mead every week or so while the spices are in it and remove them as soon as the flavor is as strong as the honey.

Hops began appearing in mead recipes around the same time their use became widespread in beer. They add a spicy, floral aroma and a distinct bitterness, which, in very modest amounts can balance the honey's sweetness. Hops also help clarify the mead and have natural preservative properties. You use hops in mead much as you do in making beer: Add bittering hops while your must is in the midst of simmering and finishing hops a few minutes before you finish simmering. Mead's flavor is more delicate than ale, so you want to be careful to introduce hops in small amounts and add more in subsequent batches if it's not hoppy enough for you.

Braggot, or mead made with malted grains, tastes more like beer and better accommodates the flavor of hops than simple mead does. Making a braggot involves preparing wort just as you would for beer—with hops added according to your taste—and adding honey before you pitch the yeast. You can work with whole-grain malts or malt extracts (learn more about these on page 107) to make braggot. Pale malt and Munich malt are two good choices for blending with honey to make braggot.

EASY SHOW MEAD

Yield: 5 gallons | OG: 1.10 | FG: 1.045 | ABV: 10 percent

INGREDIENTS
12½ pounds light honey
4 teaspoons winemaking acid blend
5 teaspoons yeast nutrient
1 package (10 grams) Sauterne wine yeast

1. Heat 2 gallons of water with the honey to 165°F and let it gently simmer at a consistent temperature for 15 minutes.
2. Remove from the heat and dissolve the acid blend in honey mixture.
3. Pour the mixture into your primary fermenter and add 3 gallons of water, or until you have 5 gallons of liquid.
4. When the mixture cools to room temperature (about 70°F), add the yeast nutrient and then pitch the started yeast.
5. Stir vigorously.
6. Cover, attach the airlock, and leave it in a cool, dark spot for two weeks, or until the bubbling of fermentation has slowed almost to a stop.
7. Rack the mead off the yeast sediment and into a carboy.
8. Set the airlock and let the mead sit for two months before racking again.
9. After two months, rack it again.
10. Two months later, check to see whether the mead is clear and the hydrometer reading is stable. If so, rack and bottle the wine. If not, rack again for another two months.
11. Wait a year—longer if you can—then enjoy with friends.

×××××××××× MEAD: THE BACKSTORY ××××××××××

EVIDENCE INDICATES THAT BEES EVOLVED RIGHT AROUND THE SAME TIME THAT flowering plants did, the Cretaceous period, about 146 to 74 million years ago. The earliest honeybee fossils are dated from about 20 million years ago. By the time mammals had supplanted dinosaurs (about twenty thousand years ago), scientists theorize, honey, water, and yeasts met up in the hollowed trees in Africa where bees nested, producing a natural mead that may well have been enjoyed by many of the creatures there, including the two-legged, upright sorts who would soon figure out how to create the safe (safer than water then), sweet, and intoxicating drink for themselves.

Pottery from northern China documents that people there were storing mead as early as 7000 BC. It is mentioned in the *Rigveda*, an ancient Indian text dating from 1700 to 1100 BC. In Greek mythology, mead was known as ambrosia, and was considered the drink of the gods. The Greeks believed it came from the heavens as dew and that bees collected it. Aristotle and Pliny the Elder both wrote more scientifically about it.

In regions where the climate suited grape growing, wine eventually supplanted mead as the most popular fermented drink. But in the colder climates of Europe, people continued to produce mead. In Norse mythology, warriors who reached Valhalla were rewarded with mead served by beautiful maidens. It had reached the British Isles in time to be mentioned in *Beowulf* and is popular still in the time of *The Canterbury Tales*. One theory on the origins of the English term *honeymoon* attributes it to the practice of the bride's father providing her with enough mead for a monthlong wedding celebration. Spiced meads were used to treat a variety of ailments, and the word *metheglin* comes from the Welsh term for "medicine."

During the medieval period, monasteries worked on perfecting the mead recipes, just as they did with ales, brandy, and other handmade spirits. As commerce increased in wine and beer, mead became less popular in most of Europe. In Scandinavia, Poland, and Russia, mead making continued into the nineteenth century. Characters in books by Tolstoy, Dostoevsky, and Gogol drink it. Today in Finland people continue to celebrate May Day with a lemon-flavored mead called *sima.* Brewing homemade mead is still widespread in Ethiopia, where it is called *tej.* The natives use the boiled leaves and bark of the *gesho*, a small indigenous tree in the buckthorn family (*Rhamnus prinioides*, to be specific), as you would hops, to add a bitter flavor to the mead.

Mead making in the United States was the passion of a few scattered aficionados and eccentrics until the late 1990s and early 2000s, when interest spiked alongside the enthusiasm for all kinds of other handcrafted food and drink. Ken Schramm's very influential book, *The Compleat Meadmaker*, and the Internet brought many of the aficionados together. A group of the leading mead makers, including Schramm, Dan McConnell, and Mike O'Brien, established the Mazer Cup International, an annual mead competition open to both professional and amateur producers. There are other international competitions and many, many regional ones you can enter, too.

More than two hundred commercial meaderies now operate across the United States, and if you don't live near one yet, you have many to choose from online. You can find meads that range from fine-wine sophisticated to in-your-face bold. Mead hasn't yet been marketed by a corporate producer, as with Woodchuck cider, but you might find white wine sweetened with honey (after fermentation) sold as "meade."

CHAPTER № 6

DARE TO DISTILL

MAKING YOUR HOMEGROWN WINE, BEER, CIDER, AND MEAD IS A deep satisfaction that grows as you gain experience and success. You can continue learning, discovering, and refining your process for as long as you live and still be challenged to ferment again. But if you want to step up to the next level or just like a stronger drink, you can use a small still in your home to create more potent spirits flavored by your own ingredients.

Fermenting captures and enhances the flavors and aromas of your homegrown ingredients and preserves them for you to enjoy for a few years. Fermented drinks continue evolving in the bottle, ideally becoming smoother along the way. They reach a peak at some time in their aging and then their flavor deteriorates, gradually at first, but eventually to the point of undrinkability. Distilling concentrates those flavors and preserves them even longer than fermenting does. The process also concentrates the alcohol content of your homemade hooch, raising it from less than 15 percent ABV (and in most cases a lot less) to 40 percent ABV or more.

The mention of a home still may conjure up associations with moonshine, illicit liquor made from corn. It's almost pure alcohol with a 95 percent ABV level (which is 190 proof). Nobody ever claims that it tastes good, but it was and is popular for the kick. You can make your own moonshine for drinking or fueling your car for backwoods racing, but that's not all you can get from a home still. You can turn your homegrown fruit and homemade wines and ciders into brandy, eau de vie (colorless fruit brandy), and more that you'll be pleased to drink and proud to share with friends.

Before we go any further, I want to be sure you understand that it is illegal everywhere in the United States, and in many other countries (except New Zealand, go figure) to distill alcohol without proper licensing. Brewing beer and making wine, cider, and mead for home consumption are not restricted (except in Alabama, go figure), but you can be prosecuted, fined, and more for distilling even just a bottle or two to enjoy yourself.

Despite the legalities, many people today are taking the risk and producing small batches of their own liquor. They are working in their kitchen, basement, and garage with stills they've built or bought, crafting unique drinks from ingredients they've sourced themselves. Many amateur distillers move up to the business of selling spirits they've made, but it can be as rewarding to do for yourself as making fermented drinks.

Distilling does take more equipment and attention than fermenting, but you don't need a lot of space or a degree in chemistry. Although not an exact comparison, the difference between fermenting and distilling is akin to that between cooking and baking. With the former, you have a recipe and a basic process, both of which you can experiment with and adapt to your tastes and ingredients. Distilling isn't very complicated, but, as with baking, you need to follow the directions precisely to get palatable results. I explain all of this not to scare you off, but to help you assess for yourself if you are ready to try.

You can distill beer and other grain mashes to make whiskey and all its variations. But the easiest, most accessible way to start distilling is with fruit-based drinks. For that reason and because you are much more likely to grow a substantial amount of fruit than grain in your garden, most of the attention in this chapter is on making brandies, eaux de vie, and the like.

⟩⟩⟩⟩⟩⟩⟩⟩⟩⟩⟩⟩⟩ THE STILL ⟨⟨⟨⟨⟨⟨⟨⟨⟨⟨⟨⟨⟨

When you distill, you don't add alcohol to wine, beer, or other drink. Rather, you simply collect the alcohol that's already present in a more concentrated form. You do this by heating up, vaporizing, and then condensing the fluid. Because water and alcohol have different boiling points, more of the latter will be in the vapor than will the former. Cooling the vapor rapidly causes the alcohol to condense, and when you gather that condensation, you have a drink that tastes like the essence of the beverage you started with.

The basic components of a still are a kettle for heating the ingredients, linked to a coil through which the vapor flows; a tube or barrel around it that is chilled (usually by water); and a tube with a spout for gathering the condensation, called a worm. The pot still is the simplest design and the most commonly used for making fruit-based liquor, especially by amateurs. The kettle may be heated directly on a burner. This allows a fair amount of control over the temperature, but you must pay careful attention to it because ingredients sitting over direct heat can burn before they vaporize. Burnt flavors are not pleasant and are just about impossible to eliminate from the finished liquor. A variation on the basic design that helps to reduce the potential for burning is to put the kettle inside a larger vessel with water that's been heated to the boiling point—like a double-boiler used for melting chocolate on your stove. Heating with water slows the distillation process and diminishes some of your control over the temperature inside the kettle but ensures that the ingredients don't have contact with direct heat. The most sophisticated stills rely on steam for heat.

Pot stills, sometimes called alembic stills, produce drinks that are in the 30 to 45 percent ABV range with lots of fruit flavor and color. To get higher and purer alcohol concentrations, you can distill the fluid again, but with each pass you lose flavor and color, and you end up with less actual liquid to drink.

You can build a simple small pot still with an ordinary household pressure cooker or other sealed stockpot-size vessel, or make a larger one with a steel beer keg or milk can. Whatever size vessel you use, it needs to be stainless steel or copper. Other metals react to the heat and to the acids in the alcohol, creating off-flavors.

Tabletop Pot Still

You also need a length of copper pipe for the condenser, a hose for getting cool water around the condenser or ice to chill the vapor, a few fittings you can buy wherever plumbing supplies are sold, and a thermometer. Remember that you need to heat the kettle, so keep in mind where and how to do that—on a stove, with a propane burner, or another heat source—when deciding what to use for the kettle. Tight-fitting welds and seals are critical for stills to prevent the vaporized alcohol from escaping before you can capture it, or worse, being ignited by your heat source. (The flammability of

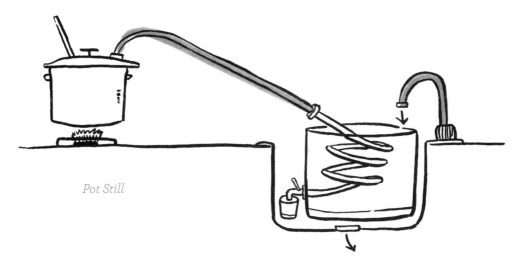

Pot Still

alcohol is one important reason why distilling is so tightly regulated.)

A manufactured still is far from necessary, and many distillers seem to relish the challenge of building a still as much as the distilling itself. But if you're not handy with solder, you should purchase a still. You'll find models that come complete with propane or electric heating elements, which can be very helpful for those living where it may not be feasible to put a large kettle on the stove for a few hours. Because of the legal issues involved, buying a pot still from a vendor in the United States is not usually as straightforward as ordering fermentation supplies. Some sources offer separate parts that you assemble, whereas others label and ship pot stills as "decorative items" or specify that the products must to be used for distilling water or extracting essential oils from herbs. A new 3-gallon pot still made from stainless steel costs less than $300 and you can find much larger ones for less than $500. Or you can convert water-distilling devices—they tend to be small (usually around 1 gallon) and they include an electric heating element.

Stainless steel and copper are efficient conductors of heat, which helps you manage the temperature of your ingredients. Stainless steel is less expensive, more durable, and easier to clean than copper, the more traditional material for stills. Copper remains popular, however, because as it heats it releases compounds that neutralize sulfides, a source of off-flavors (think sulfurous rotten eggs) that may occur in fermented drinks. Plus, copper stills also have the classic look.

The reflux still is a more advanced design that automatically distills the liquor several times, resulting in a purer, more concentrated output. A reflux still is different from a pot still in that has a tower on top, containing one or more tubes, through which the vapor rises and is partially condensed at the top. A bit of the condensation is captured and drained off, but much of it runs back down the tube onto packing, where it is revaporized and mingles with the new steam coming from the boiler. The packing is commonly stainless steel or copper mesh (like pot scrubbers), glass or ceramic. With each pass, the vapor is more thoroughly cleansed of impurities, especially by-products of fermentation (such as methanol and fusel alcohols) that mar the flavor of your finished product. The continuous distillation process, called intensification and rectification, produces drinks up to 90 percent ABV. Reflux stills take a little longer to run their cycle than pot stills do—the extra time is used to produce a more refined final product. Most moonshine stills were/are variations on the reflux design. You can buy a reflux column (as the tower is called) for less than $100 or spend several thousand on the most efficient models. You can find plans for making a reflux tower yourself, but it requires advanced welding skills and solid engineering know-how.

A fractionating still is a variation on the reflux design with a very tall tower (2 to 4 feet high). Nearly 90 percent of the vapor is condensed at the top of the tower and revaporized several times before the liquid is collected. It's necessary only if your goal is to make alcohol that's close to pure, such as isopropyl or fuel alcohol.

✕✕✕✕✕✕✕✕✕✕✕✕✕✕ INGREDIENTS ✕✕✕✕✕✕✕✕✕✕✕✕✕✕

The raw materials for your home-distilled spirits are the same as those for your wine, beer, and cider. In fact, your finished homemade wine and cider can be the actual building blocks for distilling. Or you can use your ingredients without making a finished drink first. Either way, before you can concentrate the alcohol in a still, you need to produce it. As you now know, alcohol is creating when yeasts consume sugars in the conditions they are best suited to. You can choose to distill your finished and aged fermented drinks or work with more raw fermented fruit. If you do go with one of your own wines or ciders, make sure it tastes good on its own before you distill it. The poor flavor of an inferior-tasting wine will be concentrated, not eliminated, when you distill it.

You can distill just about any type of wine, but you get the best results from those that lean toward sweetness, rather than the driest wines you've made. Grape wines are a common choice for distilling because they have an innate balance of sweet, tart, and acid flavors, which is a key reason they're so well suited to winemaking in the first place. The finest brandies, such as cognac, are made from unique blends of distilled grape wines.

Starting with freshly fermented fruit rather than aged wine is no more difficult. You simply move the ingredients from your secondary fermenter directly to the distilling kettle. The liquid you distill is referred to as the mash, and when the process is over it is called, technically speaking, distillate, which sounds a lot less fun than eau de vie (French for "water for life") or even brandy. *Marc* is the term for the pulp leftover after soft fruit is pressed and it, too, can be fermented and distilled (the spirit also is known as marc). The stems, skins, seeds, and pulp left after grapes, apples and pears are pressed is called pomace and it makes for bitter wine but delightful grappa, the traditional Italian peasant spirit. (The raw material was readily available to the poorer classes after the pure grape juice was used to make wine for wealthy people.)

After grapes, the best fruits for direct distilling are tart pie cherries (notably the Montmorency variety), European-type plums (see page 63), apricots, apples, and pears. In this case, pears are even better than apples as the flavor and aroma of the former tends to hold up through distillation better than the latter. You can use peaches, but just as with making wine, their flavor and aroma diminish during fermentation and distillation, almost to disappearing altogether. Blackberries, currants, and elderberries work better for distilling than do the less-assertive flavors of raspberries and blueberries. When fermenting the berries, be sure to add supplementary sugar to produce a strong base of alcohol content in the mash.

Picking the fruit when its sugar content is highest helps maximize its alcohol level for distilling. Overripe fruit may not have desirable eating qualities—it may be too soft or have begun to naturally ferment—but it has the most sugar at that stage and is very well suited to distilling. Stay away, though, from bruised or rotting fruit because they will bring unwelcome flavors into your mash.

Other than grapes, the fruits recommended for distilling are naturally rich in pectins that, as you may recall, bind the solids in fruit juice and make it easy for you to make jam. When distilling, pectin turns into methanol, a form of alcohol that's very potent and at too high a concentration very harmful. Later in this chapter you'll see how to reduce the methanol while distilling, but before we get there, you want to do all you can to eliminate as much pectin as possible. That begins with using pectic enzyme while preparing your must before fermentation. A valuable second step is to heat the must to 175° to 180°F for about thirty minutes before you pitch the yeast. At that temperature, the pectin breaks down and you have a liquid that will stay clearer and less viscous.

Distilling wine or plain fermented fruit juice is simplest and cleanest. But mash fermentation gets you the most flavor and aroma from the fruit. Prepare your mash as you would for making wine (as described on pages 41 to 42) but, rather than extracting the juice and leaving out the fruit's pulp and skins, merely crush the fruit to release the juice and ferment it along with the solids. And they stay with the juice throughout the fermentation period and go with it into the distillation kettle. The phenols that give fruit its taste, scent, and color vaporize along with the alcohol, infusing into the liquid as it condenses. After you're done distilling, you can compost the remaining pulp and other solids. Don't try to make wine with them again.

In describing the process of making wine, I mentioned the possibility of adding sulfites to the must to kill off naturally occurring microbes that could outcompete with yeast and spoil your results. Most experienced winemakers I have spoken to spurn the use of sulfites and rely on other strategies and strict adherence to sanitation to protect their must. But even if you do use sulfites in your winemaking, pass on it when preparing mash for distilling. The sulfur flavor and aroma become more pronounced during distillation and sulfites increase methanol production, another distinctly unappealing component in your hooch.

When grains have been malted and soaked to transform the natural starches into fermentable sugars, the result is also called mash. It is the raw material for making whiskey of all kinds. Malted barley is the predominant grain for brewing beer and for distilling into Scotch whiskey. Corn and rye are the primary ingredients in bourbon and rye whiskey. Most vodka today is made from a blend of grains, but a few distillers use the traditional potatoes as the main source of fermentable sugar. Gin also comes from distilling grain mash, but it is flavored with aromatics, specifically juniper berries. One key difference between vodka or gin and whiskey is that the latter is aged in wood, which provides much of the characteristic flavor of the various types of whiskey. Whiskey's flavor is also enhanced by filtering the alcohol through charcoal. When molasses or cane juice are fermented and then distilled, you have rum. Once you have succeeded with distilling fruit-based mash, you may find distilling with grain mash manageable and rewarding.

✕✕✕✕✕✕✕✕✕✕✕✕ DISTILLATION STEPS ✕✕✕✕✕✕✕✕✕✕✕✕

You should have gathered by now that distilling is simply a process of heating and cooling liquids. The process works because the components of fermented liquids vaporize at different temperatures. You learned in school (or should have) that water boils at 212°F when you are at sea level. At higher elevations, where atmospheric pressure is lower, water boils at a lower temperature. At any elevation, water may begin to vaporize before it reaches the boiling point, particularly when the ambient humidity level is low. At sea level and moderate humidity levels, methanol vaporizes at about 150°F, whereas the ethyl alcohol you want to capture begins turning to steam at about 175°F.

Your still is most efficient and produces the most valuable results when the mash stays as long as possible around 175°F. This is most easily managed with a moderate amount of mash—for a home still, that's probably no more than about 2 gallons at a time. You may be tempted to go for more and produce faster, but unless you have a sophisticated still apparatus, you're better off working with smaller batches. You can expect to get about 2 quarts of drinkable spirits from 2 gallons of mash.

Start by putting your mash in the kettle—fill it only about halfway to leave room for foam that some ingredients produce. If your mash is very thick with pulp and other solids, add a little distilled water so that it is the consistency of chunky soup. Begin heating it gradually (fast heating promotes burning). As the temperature rises, condensed liquid begins to drip out of the spout, which you can catch with a glass or bottle. The first cup or so that you get is known as the heads of the distillate. It is mostly methanol, which vaporizes at the lower temperature. Discard the methanol—it tastes nasty and it's this element that can cause the temporary blindness attributed to moonshine.

As the mash's temperature moves into the range where ethyl alcohol vaporizes (again, 175°F), you can begin to capture what is called the hearts of the distillate, the liquor you're trying to produce. It comes out in a steady flow. The mash may continue producing hearts for a half-hour or more, so you want to keep the temperature as steady as possible and capture as much of it as you can.

As the amount of liquid in the kettle diminishes, the mash's temperature rises and the water, fusel alcohol, and other components of the liquid vaporize. This last portion of the distillate is called tails. These are often returned to the still to run through again, where they can be further purified. For the finest-quality spirit, discard the tails.

The most reliable way to tell when the heads turn to hearts and the hearts turn to tails is with a thermometer inside the mash kettle. As the internal temperature passes 170°F, the ethyl alcohol begins to vaporize and the stream coming out of the still grows stronger and steadier. Hold the temperature in that range for as long as you can to maximize the amount you get. When mash is warmer than 185°F, the fusel alcohol and water start vaporizing, and you are collecting the tails.

You can perform a simple, mostly accurate test to assess what you've captured, with a spoon and a butane lighter. Spoon up a little of the distillate and light it. Methanol produces an almost invisible flame, ethyl alcohol makes a blue flame, and fusel alcohol burns yellow.

You can bottle the hearts of the distillation and have a fruity liquor to share. Many distillers, however, take the so-called coarse spirits and distill them a second time to purify it to create a fine spirit. The latter has a smoother taste because you have further separated the ethyl alcohol from the other components; and a higher alcohol by volume, because you have further concentrated it. But less of the flavor and aroma compounds make it through this second stage, making your liquor more like odorless, nearly flavorless vodka. And you may end up with 20 percent less drinkable liquid.

The liquor you have captured from your still is likely to be strong in flavor and alcohol content. Sip it before you bottle it to see how it tastes and feels. You may find, as many home distillers do, that you need to add water to each serving to make your drink palatable. You can dilute according to your own preferences, but a general rule of thumb is to mix one part water to two parts liquor.

Unlike wine, mead, cider, or beer, homemade liquor can be bottled in just about any glass container you like. Mason jars are classic moonshine containers, but your friends might find your brandy or eau de vie more appealing in a proper bottle. It needs to be clean, of course, but sterilizing isn't as important as it is with fermented drinks. The distilling process and the high alcohol content of spirits kill off bacteria and other microbes that cause spoilage. Aging your home-distilled spirits is not necessary, but letting it rest for a few days after distilling often helps to smooth out the flavor. Before you drink them, you can infuse them with homegrown fruit and herbs—find out more about that in the next chapter.

POTATO VODKA

Potatoes, the staple food of people in Eastern Europe, also were the primary ingredient in vodka, their traditional drink. Although today corn, wheat, or other grains are the main ingredient in nearly all commercial brands of vodka, making it with potatoes you've grown yourself is no more challenging than distilling fruit-based liquor.

GROWING SPUDS. Potatoes grow underground, but you don't need a large garden plot or any at all to raise enough to make a few batches of vodka. If you don't have space in the garden for potatoes, you can plant them in a large burlap bag or even a plastic trash can with a few airholes punched in it. You'll also need a blend of equal parts compost and peat for growing them in one of those containers, or just compost when planting them in the ground.

This year's potatoes grow from pieces of last year's tubers, sometimes called seed potatoes. The eyes, or little sproutlets, on a potato grow new roots when planted; and from those roots, the new spuds are formed. You can cut up a potato you bought at the supermarket for your seeds, if the potato has not been treated with an antisprouting agent (if no sproutlets emerge from the eyes when you keep the potato in the dark for a few weeks, it has been treated). More reliable sources for seed potatoes are local farmers, garden centers, or mail-order suppliers. Wherever you get the seed potatoes from,

Growing Potatoes

be sure each one you plant has at least one eye. The best varieties for making vodka are those with the highest starch content, such as russets and other baking types, because they yield the most fermentable sugar. Small, red, or yellow potatoes tend to have the least amount of starch and are better for roasting than distilling.

The best time to plant potatoes is about a month before your last frost date in spring. To grow them in the ground, dig a trench 8 to 10 inches deep and about 6 inches across. For growing in a container, put 8 inches or so of the compost/peat blend in the bottom of the bag or can. In both cases, set the seed potatoes on top of the soil (or compost/peat) and cover them with more soil so they are about 3 inches deep. Water well. In a week or so, the seed potatoes start sprouting a tall green stalk above ground. As the stalk grows, add more soil on top of the potatoes so that only the stalk is visible. Continue adding soil, making sure that none of the potato is ever exposed to sunlight. (When the sun hits the tubers, they start to turn green and develop a mild toxin that makes the potatoes unpalatable.) Keep the soil moist but not soggy. In six to eight weeks, your container or trench will be full of soil and the stalk will look a lot like a tomato plant (they're closely related to potatoes)—it will be 2 to 3 feet tall, have a canopy of branches and leaves, and eventually small yellow flowers.

When the stalk begins to yellow and dry down, about three months after planting them, your potatoes are ready to harvest. If you've grown them in your garden, carefully dig them up, taking care not to damage them with your shovel. Harvesting potatoes from a container is even easier and kind of fun. Simply dump out the container onto the ground and sift through the soil for the buried treasure, your homegrown spuds. You can expect to harvest 10 to 15 pounds of potatoes—about what you need to make 1 gallon of vodka—from each container or 8-foot-long row.

MASHING POTATOES. If you were planning to eat your potatoes, I would recommend that you let them sit for a few days in a cool, dark place to give their skins a chance to toughen up a bit and their flesh time to dry out a bit. For making vodka, however, you can and should use fresh potatoes as soon as possible.

Start by cleaning the potatoes well, then cutting them into chunks. As you do this, you will discover what makes home-grown potatoes better than store-bought: Your fresh potatoes are very juicy, and for that reason, they're well suited to making vodka. Put the potato chunks in a large stockpot and cover with water. Gradually bring the water to a boil and let simmer for an hour, stirring occasionally so the potatoes don't stick to the pot or one another.

When the hour is up, turn off the heat and allow the potatoes to cool. Gently mash the potatoes in the water until you have a starchy slurry. Potatoes, unlike grains, do not naturally contain enzymes that convert starches to fermentable sugars. You have two choices for introducing those enzymes: Add malted grains to your mash (page 107) or purchase packets of amalyse enzymes from brewing suppliers or a health food store. Whichever you choose, add the malt or packet of enzyme to the potato slurry, then pour it into a mashing tun or a large stockpot and heat to 150°F. Add about 1 pound of malted grain for each 5 pounds of potatoes you started with. (Follow the instructions if you go with the packaged enzymes.) Keep the pot over low heat so that the temperature remains at 150°F for two hours, the ideal conditions for activating the enzymes.

Let the mash cool and leave it to sit (covered) overnight, allowing the enzymes to continue breaking down the starch. The next day, pour the contents into a fermentation bucket, add an equal volume of water and mix well. You can buy so-called turbo yeasts or other yeasts selected for distilling, but you can use any strain that has a high alcohol tolerance. Use one packet (10 grams) of yeast for up to 5 gallons of mash. Pitch the yeast the day after you've made the mash and allow five to seven days for it to ferment. When fermentation is done (few bubbles in the airlock), the mash is ready for your still. Finish making your vodka by distilling it as you would fruit mash (page 163). If you are using a pot still, take the time to distill the potato liquor at least twice; three times is even better.

When the distillation is over, most commercial producers filter their vodka through charcoal to further purify it. You can buy a filter kit; an ordinary water purification pitcher with a charcoal cartridge (such as the Brita brand) also works. The finished vodka is ready for infusing with other flavors or blending into cocktails.

FOND OF ABSINTHE

As colorful as the history and mythology of moonshine is, absinthe's may be even more lurid. The herb-flavored and herb-tinted liquor was known as the "Green Fairy" and developed a following among the artists, writers and other bohemians living in France in the late nineteenth and early twentieth centuries. Its devotees claimed that it promoted visions, that it was more psychoactive than mere alcohol. It was reported that Van Gogh cut off his ear under the deranging influence of absinthe. Even ordinary drinkers prepared it according to a set of rituals and it was reputed to be highly addictive. By 1915, it had caught the attention of advocates for temperance, and making, selling, and drinking absinthe were outlawed in the United States and most Western European countries. Although no reliable data ever showed that absinthe possessed powers beyond those of any strong liquor, the ban remained in effect until the 1990s, when it was rediscovered by adventurous drinkers, who lobbied for changes in the law. Today, hundreds of commercial brands are available, ranging from artisan-crafted bottles that cost hundreds of dollars to cheap imitations made with artificially flavored and colored vodka.

When made properly, absinthe is a combination of an infusion (which are covered in more detail in the next chapter) and distillation. You can try to approximate the flavor of absinthe by just infusing it—and you may create an enjoyable drink—but distilling concentrates the characteristic flavors. More on that in a bit—first, let's get into the herbs that produce absinthe's unique taste and color.

HERBAL MEDLEY. Absinthe may seem like an exotic drink, but the flavoring ingredients are anything but. You can grow all of them in a small garden or even in pots on a patio, just about anywhere except the most extreme climates of North America. The defining herb in absinthe is wormwood, known to botanists as *Artemisia absinthium*. It's important to know that because there are other plants commonly called wormwood that do not have the same flavors and aromas. Wormwood has long been used as a medicinal plant—absinthe was created by a Swiss doctor in the 1790s, who was trying to prepare a remedy with it. Thujone is a compound found in many plants, but wormwood releases its supply when it soaks in alcohol. Absinthe's exceptional properties usually are attributed to thujone. If you rub the leaves on your skin on a summer night, you will find that wormwood also works as an insect repellent. (Unfortunately, no studies have been published addressing the proposition that drinking absinthe repels insects.)

Wormwood is a perennial that grows into a small shrub—it reaches 1 to 3 feet tall, with thin, silvery green serrated leaves and round yellow flowers in midsummer. It is very drought tolerant and often is found growing wild along roadsides and other uncultivated areas. Harvest the leaves anytime, though they are richest in the all-important essential oils in the spring, when the leaves are young. You can start a patch of wormwood with seeds or transplants in spring after all danger of frost has passed. Like just about all herbs, including the others that go into absinthe, wormwood needs very well-drained soil and full sun, except in the hottest, driest climates (where a little shade can help protect them). Thujone does have one very noteworthy property—the compound leaches from the roots into the surrounding soil and suppresses the growth of many other plants. Plant wormwood away from your vegetable garden, as it affects tomatoes, strawberries, and many other popular crops. Wormwood isn't lethal if ingested, but it got its name as a treatment for parasitic worms and you don't want to experience worm-purging unless absolutely necessary.

The other herbs in absinthe may vary, but almost always include fennel, anise, mint, lemon balm (*Melissa officinalis*), chamomile, and angelica. Hyssop and coriander are also frequently used. All of these herbs are best started with transplants in spring. Mint, and its relatives lemon balm and hyssop, are aggressive and can become garden bullies, crowding out other plants you want to grow. One way to control that tendency is to plant them in a pot and then bury the pot almost to its edge. For flavoring your absinthe, you strip and crush the leaves of mint, lemon balm, and hyssop, and the flowers of chamomile. Pull the roots of angelica and gather the seeds of fennel, anise, and coriander—break the seeds open in a coffee grinder or food processor to help release their flavors.

THE INFUSION. The base for homemade absinthe is Everclear grain alcohol, unflavored vodka, or any liquor that's 85 percent ABV. In a large clean jar or any glass container with a large mouth, put an ounce of crushed wormwood leaves and cover them with 2 quarts of the liquor, shake gently, and store in a cool, dark place for ten days to two weeks, shaking gently about once a day. When the liquor has a light greenish tint and smells strongly bitter, filter out the wormwood. Add a tablespoon of each of the other herbs to the wormwood infusion, shake it gently, and wait another couple of days for their flavors to infuse.

FILTER AND DILUTE. Strain out the plant matter—a coffee filter works well for this. Mix water with your infusion at about a five-to-one ratio. If you just want a drink that has a taste reminiscent of absinthe and don't want to bother with distilling, you can let the infusion rest for a day or two to further blend the herbs' flavors, and then drink it.

DISTILL. For a more authentic absinthe, distill the infusion just as if you are making brandy or eau de vie. Take extra care not to let the herbs burn while you are heating the mash, by raising the temperature gradually—they can char quickly over direct flame.

COLOR AND AGE. Divide the absinthe distillate that you've gathered into two equal parts. To one part, add another ounce of wormwood; and to the other, about a tablespoon each of the other herbs (crush the leaves of the mint, lemon balm, and hyssop). Allow both parts to infuse for two to three days—the one with the mixed herbs should be vivid green. Strain out the herbs and mix the two parts together again. Leave the flavors to blend for two weeks before you drink your absinthe.

SERVE. The final step before drinking absinthe is the ritual known as La Louche. It involves both further diluting and sweetening the bitter drink. Some believe it's the secret to unlocking its purported powers or at least the best way to activate the essential oils in the herbs. To perform the ritual in classic fashion, you need a glass with a reservoir at the bottom, a slotted spoon, sugar cubes, and about twice as much ice-cold water as absinthe. You fill the reservoir with a couple of ounces of absinthe, rest the spoon on the top of the glass, and put two sugar cubes on the spoon. As you slowly pour the water over the sugar, it melts and drips into the absinthe, changing the drink's color from emerald green to milky, cloudy green and eventually to an opalescent light green. In a recent variation on this ritual, popularized in the Czech Republic, the sugar cubes are soaked in absinthe before they are set on the spoon and then they are ignited. The sugar caramelizes and drips into the drink as it is cooled by the water. Dramatic stuff, but not nearly as exciting as drinking absinthe you've made yourself from homegrown ingredients.

XXXXXXXXXXXXXXX SPOTLIGHT ON: XXXXXXXXXXXXXXX
WARWICK VALLEY WINERY AND DISTILLERY

JASON GRIZZANTI AND JEREMY KIDDE HAVE BEEN FRIENDS SINCE THEY WERE growing up in New York's Hudson River Valley, and they stayed in touch even after Grizzanti went to Cornell University to major in pomology (the study of tree fruit) and Kidde moved to the Bay Area for his work in finance. A few years later, Grizzanti asked Kidde to come back to New York State and work together on a property his family was not using.

"The property had an apple orchard, but some members of the family had tried to start a winery on it," Grizzanti says. "The Hudson Valley is a great place to grow apples, but even the best grapes here will never rival those from the West Coast.

"We produce a few wines, but we found our real calling when we started making hard cider. We tasted a lot of other ciders from New York and found few, if any, that were worth drinking. For that reason, we encountered a lot of skepticism when we started selling ours."

They purchased the orchard in 1989 and started selling in 1994, but it still took a few years after, they admit, to produce truly worthy beverages. With Grizzanti's expertise on fruit growing and Kidde's business savvy, they began making and marketing Doc's Draft Hard Apple Cider, Hard Pear Cider, and Hard Raspberry Cider, which began earning positive reviews and competition awards almost immediately. By 2001, they were ready for next challenge.

"We became the first micro-distillery licensed in New York State since Prohibition," Kidde says. "We felt there was a lot of potential for distilled products once public perception changed about the other items we were offering." Their American Fruits label includes black currant and sour cherry cordials, as well as apple and pear brandies. They also now offer their own Warwick Gin, made from ingredients they grow or source locally.

"Making cider, wine, and distilled liquor is not magic, it's science," Grizzanti says. "You need to understand that science to get good results.

"To make truly great drinks, however, is an art," he adds, "learned over many hours and many failures."

✕✕✕✕✕✕✕✕✕ DISTILLING: THE BACKSTORY ✕✕✕✕✕✕✕✕✕

THE FIRST APPLICATION OF THE DISTILLATION PROCESS WAS LIKELY NOT TO MAKE spirits; rather, to extract and concentrate the essential oils of herbs to use as medicine. The earliest civilizations had discovered how to use heat to condense and then separate alcohol from water and other components, and by 800 BC, the Chinese were already drinking spirits made from rice. The ancient Greeks and Romans, as well as the Middle Eastern cultures, distilled wine to make brandylike beverages.

The history of whiskey and other grain-based spirits is not as clear, though the process for making them was standardized in Scotland or Ireland more than five hundred years ago, when it was first mentioned in written records. Rum was one critical leg in the triangle of trade that brought African slaves to American colonies and the Caribbean (molasses to make the rum, and the slaves to work the sugar plantations, were the other two components). For ordinary people, apple jack was the most prevalent spirit in the American colonies, but whiskey became a very important commodity. It played a critical role in the first test of the new federal government's authority after the Constitution was adopted. In 1791, Congress levied a new excise tax on whiskey. It prompted a revolt, later known as the Whiskey Rebellion, by farmers on the western side of the Allegheny Mountains, who processed their grain into a more valuable and less perishable product, liquor. President George Washington led a militia of fifteen thousand troops to the area near current-day Pittsburgh, to put down the revolt. No shots were fired, the rebels dispersed, and the new political party headed by Thomas Jefferson repealed the tax just a few years later.

When Prohibition was enacted in the late nineteenth and early twentieth centuries, distillers went underground, producing moonshine whiskey primarily in rural areas, and bathtub gin in cities. After Prohibition and in the years after, corporations supplied most of the liquor consumed in the United States, and still do. But in the last twenty years, small-batch, artisanal distilling has enjoyed a revival like that of craft brewing. It is easier than ever to find unique distilled drinks made with local, seasonal ingredients. Distilling remains illegal without a license, even for personal consumption, so there are no reliable statistics on the number of amateur distillers, but a growing number of chefs, bartenders, and enthusiasts are discreetly making all kinds of high-quality liquors for themselves, family, and friends.

JACKED APPLE CIDER

Calvados is a highly refined apple brandy that, like Champagne and Burgundy, comes from one specific region of France—in this case, a few *departements* (like counties in the United States) in Normandy. As many as one hundred different varieties of apples are used to make Calvados, always including sweet, sharp, and bitter types. Cider pears may also be a part of the blend. According to French regulations, the cider used to make Calvados must be fermented for no less than six weeks and it is typically distilled in alembic (or pot) stills. After distillation, the brandy is aged for at least two years in oak barrels. When finished, the alcohol content can be as high as 72 percent ABV. Potent stuff.

You don't have to move to France or adhere to specific regulations to turn homemade apple cider into strong, apple-flavored liquor. In fact, you don't even need a still to make traditional apple jack, the most widely available spirit during America's colonial period. In those days, it was sometimes called Jersey Lightning, perhaps because one of the colonies' largest producers was based there. Even after commercial production began, many families living in New England and other frigid winter climates made their own.

The standard base ingredient for apple jack is apple wine, though you can use homemade hard cider, too. The most important difference between the two is that apple wine has been fermented with added sugar and as a result has a higher ABV than cider—10 to 12 percent ABV versus 4 to 6 percent. Tannins are an important flavor component in apple jack. If you don't have cider apple varieties, which are naturally high in tannins, include crab apples (which are easy to grow or forage for in most cities and suburbs; see page 137) in your blend.

Transforming apple wine or cider into apple jack could not be simpler, using a method known as freeze distillation. You don't need a still, just a freezer or a few weeks of subfreezing temperatures outside. After the wine or cider has fermented and then rested for a couple of weeks, you put it in the freezer or outside when temperatures are consistently below the freezing mark.

Do not use a glass bottle for this. Not only will it make it hard to do the next step, glass breaks easily when frozen and that can leave quite a mess in your freezer. Any clean, food-safe plastic container works, including a fermentation bucket or other sturdy container with a wide opening and a lid. If you would like to go the traditional route, our forebears made apple jack in wooden barrels.

Just as standard distilling relies on the different properties of alcohol and water to separate them, so does freeze distillation, only at the opposite end of the temperature spectrum. Water freezes at a higher temperature than alcohol, and as it does it rises to the top of the liquid. As you remove the ice, the amount of water is decreased and the alcohol content and apple flavor are concentrated in the liquid. At 32°F, ice will form at the top until the remaining liquid is 14 percent ABV. Lower the temperature to 14°F and ice continues forming until 20 percent of the volume is alcohol. If you can get it as cold as –4°F (not easy to do unless you live where winter temperatures stay below zero or you have access to a commercial freezer), you will have a drink that's 27 percent ABV, and at –22°F, it will be 33 percent ABV.

After two days in the deep freeze, begin to check your fermented apple drink each day and scoop off any ice that has formed. Within a few days, you will note that less and less ice is forming. You can take the apple jack out of the freezer and begin to drink it at any time you want, but to continue concentrating the alcohol content and flavor, you need to gradually lower the temperature. Your homemade apple jack has reached its full potential and is ready to drink and share when you find no more ice on top.

Although freeze distillation is the traditional way to make apple jack, it works with just about any wine or mead you've made.

CHAPTER 7

INTERESTING INFUSIONS

THE EASIEST AND FASTEST WAY TO TURN FRESH HOMEGROWN INGREDI-ents into your own adult beverages is to use them in infusions that you can serve by themselves or blend into cocktails. In this case, you're not making alcohol but giving it your own unique flavor. It's so simple that in many cases all you need to do is soak your ingredients in wine or spirits. In just a few days or weeks, you can have results that are ready to share.

✕✕✕✕✕✕✕✕✕✕✕ FLAVORED VODKAS ✕✕✕✕✕✕✕✕✕✕✕

Vodka used to be the plainest of drinks—clear, odorless, and tasting of little but alcohol. But in recent years, the shelves at your local liquor have filled up with a wide variety of vodkas in flavors ranging from lemon and chile pepper to chocolate, birthday cake, and s'mores. Nearly all of those are made with artificial flavorings that are designed to replicate the taste of real food.

You don't have to settle for fake flavors or pay the premium for such enhanced vodka. You take fresh ingredients from your garden and transform ordinary vodka into something new and different. You can also easily infuse gin, sake, or light rum. The more pronounced flavors of darker liquors make them less open to infusions of other tastes, though you may find a blend with brandy or even whiskey that you like. Whichever type of liquor you choose, remember that your homemade drinks can only taste as good as their weakest ingredients. Cheap, low-quality alcohol tends to have harsh aftertastes that will not be covered up by the flavors of the infused ingredients. That isn't to say you need to buy the most expensive bottles, but beware of the bargain-basement brands.

The quick results and ease of making infusions let you experiment often to find the right combinations for your taste and the concentrations that work best. When choos-

ing how much of your ingredients to use with the liquor, start with this rule of thumb in mind: Use about 3 cups of produce for each quart of liquor. Mason jars are the most convenient vessels for making infusions, but you can use any thoroughly cleaned glass container with an opening wide enough to allow you to put in the ingredients, and a lid that fits. Avoid using plastic containers because the alcohol may absorb odors and flavors that tend to cling to plastic even after it's been washed.

Put your fresh ingredients in the jar first and then pour in the alcohol. With the lid on, gently shake or turn over the jar several times. Repeat that once or twice a day during the infusion period. Although it can be fun to look at and showcase your infusions to visitors, you want to store them in a cool place away from direct sunlight. As you reach the suggested infusion period, begin to sample the drink and assess its flavor. You want the taste to be noticeable, but not to overpower the drink. Be patient, as it can take some ingredients two weeks or more to permeate the alcohol. When you are content with the flavor, strain out the ingredients through a cheesecloth—it's ideal because it captures the tiniest particles that float loose from many ingredients. Coffee filters or a fine kitchen strainer also work well.

INGREDIENT OPTIONS

FRESH BERRIES are a natural first choice for infusions. Blueberries, blackberries, raspberries, strawberries, gooseberries, and currants each have a unique taste and the fruits' sweetness complements and softens the sharper flavor of alcohol. You'll find detailed information on growing berries and harvesting them at the peak of ripeness in Chapter 2. Before you use them in an infusion, be sure to rinse them well, remove any stems that came along with the berries (stems have a bitter taste) and discard every berry that is shriveled or has even the slightest hint of mold on it, which can leave all of the liquor tasting as if it has spoiled.

Strawberries need to be sliced in half or into quarters before you use them in an infusion. Be sure to cut off all of the green leaves. You can put in all of the other berries whole. Steep the berries in the alcohol for no less than one week, but in most cases you will want to wait two to three weeks. If you find that the flavor is not reaching the saturation level you want, you can strain out the old fruit and replace it with fresh berries. Strawberries tend to turn almost white when all of their flavor and aroma has leached into the alcohol. At that point, you can either be content with the infusion or continue infusing with fresh fruit. You can create an infusion with a classic spring flavor by including chunks of rhubarb stalk with strawberries. Rhubarb is a perennial crop (so you plant it once and it comes back year after year) with a tangy taste. Be sure to use only the stalks—the leaves are mildly toxic—and let it continue to infuse for another week after you remove the berries.

ORCHARD FRUITS such as peaches, plums, apricots, and cherries are almost as easy as berries to use in infusions, though growing these ingredients demands more time and space (see pages 61 to 67). The flavors and aromas of tree fruits blend well with alcohol, while holding on to their fresh-picked taste.

To use peaches, plums, and apricots, cut them open to remove the pit, then slice them into thin wedges. Leave the skins on, but be sure to pare off any brown spots on the fruit. For cherries, simply cut in half, remove the pit, and they're ready to use. A week of infusing is almost always sufficient for plums and cherries; milder-tasting peaches and apricots yield more flavor after a second week.

A semitropical climate is ideal for raising CITRUS FRUIT, but you can harvest enough lemons, limes, and even grapefruits for infusions from dwarf trees grown in containers in sunny spots in almost any region, to make your own refreshing limoncello. (See pages 70 to 73 for all about growing citrus.) After you've harvested the fruit, you want to extract the essential oils in the rind for your infusions. The oils are potent flavors that are highlighted in alcohol. Use a grater like a Microplane or vegetable peeler to carve off strips of the rind. Stay close to the surface of the rind with your grater to avoid getting the pale, dry pith along with the outer skin—the pith has a bitter flavor that becomes even more pronounced in the infusion. When you have a few cups of the peeled or grated rind, lightly squeeze them to bring the essential oils to the surface. After a couple of weeks in alcohol, the rind strips become stiff and the oils have passed from them to the liquid. Many people find that cooling citrus-infused alcohol to freezing temperatures before you drink it further concentrates the infusion's flavor.

SUMMER GARDEN CROPS SUCH AS WATERMELONS, CANTALOUPES, AND CUCUMBERS (all closely related members of the squash family) don't require the long-term commitment to grow that berries and orchard fruits demand, though you do need at least 40 square feet of garden space for watermelon vines to spread out and bear fruit. Cantaloupes need less room and you can (and should) grow cucumber vines on a trellis that takes up vertical rather than horizontal space. The specifics on growing and harvesting them are on pages 79 to 83.

I remember a summer party or two during my college years when the host injected (yes, using a hypodermic needle) a whole watermelon with vodka or maybe grain alcohol. Biting into a piece of that watermelon could hit you with an almost straight shot of sweetened liquor or you might just get a hint of the alcohol. An infusion made with watermelon is a more balanced—and more civilized, I suppose—way to enjoy the refreshing flavor of the melon. With its extra sweet flavor and juiciness, watermelon is very well suited to making a quick and refreshing infusion. And it turns the liquor a very summery hue. That color can be a pastel pink or light sunny yellow, depending on whether you choose a red- or yellow-fleshed melon. There is not much difference in taste or in how they grow, so you can base your choice on your personal preference. Or you can grow some of each. To make the infusion, start by slicing the flesh off the rind and cutting it into chunks. Watermelon pulp almost dissolves during the brief infusion period of two to three days. Strain out any remaining pulp and seeds, and serve it alone over ice.

Cantaloupe is not quite as sweet and juicy as watermelon but it works almost as well in an infusion. It is certain to have more authentic flavor than the almost syrupy taste of those green melon liqueurs you find in stores. To prepare cantaloupe for infusion, cut it open and scrape out the seeds and stringy pulp attached to them. Cut the flesh from the rind and then into rough chunks to put into the alcohol. The pulp won't quite dissolve as watermelon does, but it will tint the liquor a light orange color. Let it steep for four to five days before you strain it out.

Cucumbers have a high water content and their flavor can be very subtle, but they impart very refreshing, light taste to an infusion. They work especially well in gin. I explain the differences between slicing and pickling cucumber varieties on page 79; both can be used for infusions, though the less seedy picklers have a stronger cucumber flavor. Much of that flavor is in the outer skin, which you do not need to remove if you've grown the cucumbers yourself or purchased them from a farmers' market. Remove the skin of cucumbers from supermarkets because they have been coated with wax to preserve them. Slice any cucumber you're using at least $1/4$ inch thick before putting them into an infusion, so they hold together as they steep. To get the most of their flavor, leave them in the alcohol for two weeks. Remove the cucumbers if they begin to look translucent and wilted. Adding lemon rind to an infusion helps to bring out the cucumbers' flavor.

CHILE PEPPERS make a spicy infusion that can be the foundation for a spunky Bloody Mary or other cocktails that benefit from a little heat. (You can find out more about growing your own chiles on pages 79 to 83.) Whether you prefer the sinus-burning strength of habanero peppers or the mild tingle of jalapeños, you want to leave the peppers on the plant until they reach their fully ripe color of red, orange, or yellow. At that stage, they have their complete complement of flavors, which emerge through the heat and add depth to your infusion. Removing the peppers' seeds and inner ribs reduces the heat a little. Whether you want to go seedless or not, slice the peppers in half to allow their essential oils to permeate the infusion, which rarely takes more than two to three days.

GARLIC-infused vinegars and oils are useful ingredients for making salad dressings, stir-fries, and other dishes that benefit from its pungent flavor. Drinking a garlic infusion may not sound as appealing, but the subtle taste can perk up a Bloody Mary, Dirty Martini, or many of the new savory cocktails that have become popular in recent years. Growing your own garlic is as easy as growing daffodils. To start, get whole garlic bulbs in late summer or early fall from a local grower or at the farmers' market. (Supermarket garlic is typically treated with an antisprouting agent that keeps it from growing in your garden.) If you have a choice, hardneck varieties of garlic are more widely adapted to the different climate zones of North America than are softneck types. After loosening the soil at least 6 inches down, plant individual cloves at that depth and at least 12 inches apart. Set them so that the pointy end is up. Cover the cloves with soil and a layer of straw or grass clipping mulch and water well. Each clove sprouts up a green stalk in autumn. It goes dormant in winter and begins growing again when warm weather returns. In early summer, the stalk turns yellow and begins to dry, indicating the garlic is finishing its life cycle. When the stalks are fully yellow, carefully dig them up and let them cure in a cool, dark spot for a week or two with the stalks attached. Then you can trim off the stalks and little white roots and begin enjoying your garlic harvest. To use them in an infusion, remove the papery skin from a couple of cloves and steep them in alcohol for about four days.

HERBS enhance the flavor of food and do the same for drinks. You can use such herbs as parsley, cilantro, basil, lemongrass, mint, and lavender in cocktails, and they also infuse simply and swiftly, too. Growing them is almost as easy. They require little more than a minimum of four hours or more of direct sunlight a day and soil that drains well. They grow best from started plants rather than seeds. Parsley and cilantro fare well in the cooler temperatures of spring, but you want to plant the others after the danger of frost has passed in spring. There's no need to fertilize any herbs. Snipping off a few sprigs whenever you need them actually stimulates them to keep growing and producing more. If you do not have outdoor growing space, most herbs (lavender is a notable exception) grow abundantly in containers. Even in winter they thrive and bear new leaves if you keep the pots on a sunny, south- or west-facing windowsill. One note of caution: Mint can be a very aggressive in a garden, quickly spreading via underground roots to spots far from where you planted it. To control this, plant mint in a pot and then set the pot in a hole you've dug in the ground.

When you're ready to use your herbs in an infusion, cut a few stems with leaves attached and gently crush them before steeping them in alcohol. The flavor of fresh herbs infuses into alcohol in two weeks; if you use dried herbs, you may need to wait a month or more for the infusion to get the herb's taste.

Rose hips are actually the fruit of rose bushes, and they taste like tart berries. The hips form after the rose's flower and the petals fall off, typically in midsummer (spring-blooming varieties) or early fall (all-season bloomers). When the hips are plump and brilliant orange, clip them off and remove any leaf and stem still attached to them. Cut them in half before putting them in your infusion jar and adding the alcohol. The subtle flavor takes about three weeks to infuse the drink.

HOME-STYLE AQUAVIT

The traditional drink of Scandinavians, aquavit starts out very much like vodka—a spirit distilled from either grain or potatoes. Aquavit, however, is always infused with herbs, spices, or fruit. The flavorings in classic aquavit vary depending on the specific country of origin, but they often include caraway, cardamom, cumin, coriander, anise, fennel, dill, and citrus. There are, though, many variations that include fruit, such as apples, raspberries, or plums; and herbs and spices such as mint, lemon verbena, cinnamon, or ginger.

You can make a mock aquavit with vodka and fresh ingredients you have grown yourself. Cinnamon, cardamom, and cloves require a semitropical climate, but if you have a three- to four-month growing season—that is, between 90 and 120 days each year without a hard freeze—you can grow many of the other flavorings for aquavit in your garden or in containers. For information on growing ginger, see page 119; earlier in this chapter, I covered how to grow mint (which, truth be told, is a lot easier than trying not to grow mint once you've started). Right here, we'll delve into a few spices you can grow yourself and use to flavor aquavit.

ANISE is a bushy plant that grows up to 2 feet tall and wide. It is very sensitive to cold, so you need to wait until after the danger of frost has passed in spring before you plant the seeds directly in your garden. If your growing season is not quite three months long, you can plant the seeds indoors in a plastic tray under ordinary fluorescent shop lights about four weeks before your last frost and then move the little seedlings outdoors when the weather has warmed up. Anise plants need at least six hours of direct sunlight to reach their full size, bloom, and produce the seeds you want for your infusion. You can plant anise in a large pot and move it into the sunlight, if you don't have a suitable spot in your garden. In midsummer, the plant opens clusters of small, yellow-white flowers that turn to seeds as the growing season winds down. The flower stalks turn yellow to brown when the seeds are fully mature. You can cut off the stalks and remove the seeds simply by rubbing them with your hands. Rub them over a large bowl to capture the seeds. If you live where winters are not too long and frigid, leave a flower stalk or two on the plant and the following season you are likely to see new anise plants coming up in your garden.

CARAWAY SEEDS are the flavoring most commonly associated with aquavit (as well as the best rye bread). They are harvested from a plant that has a biennial life cycle, which means it takes two growing seasons to mature and bear seeds. You can plant the seeds directly in your garden or in a large container in spring or early fall, because caraway survives winter in most of North America. Caraway plants grow about 8 inches in their first year and reach 2 feet tall by the time they get to full size in the early summer of the second season. Once they are mature, they bear clusters of small flowers with white petals and a yellow eye. The pollinated flowers produce the seeds. As with anise, when the flower stalks are brown you can cut them off and rub them over a pan or bowl to harvest the seeds.

CORIANDER SEEDS come from the same plant as the herb cilantro, an essential ingredient in salsa and many other Mexican dishes. Because it grows best in cool conditions, you can plant it in spring or early fall. Many herb growers insist that you must start the plant by sowing seeds directly in your garden or a pot because it suffers when you transplant seedlings, but I've had no trouble with that. Once the plant begins producing a steady flush of leaves, you can start snipping them off and eating them, as long as you don't take more than one-third of them at a time. When the daylight hours reach their peak in summer and the temperatures stay warmer than about 75°F, cilantro stops making new leaves and grows a stalk that blooms with tiny white flowers. The blooms turn to tight little buds that, when brown at the end of the season, yield the seeds. After cutting off the flowers, pinching the buds between your thumb and forefinger extracts the seeds.

CUMIN is a semitropical plant that can grow and produce its flavorful seeds during the summer in temperate climates. The black, white, and amber varieties are very similar in their growth habits, though some say the black are the most flavorful. If you don't have four months without frost, start cumin seeds indoors in a tray six to eight weeks before your climate warms up for good in spring. Where you do have a long growing season, you can plant cumin seeds directly in your garden or in a medium-size container. The plant grows to about a foot tall and the thin stems are prone to falling over when the heavy seed pods form in late summer. A dense stand of cumin plants can lean against one another to stay upright, but to ensure you get a full harvest of the seeds, support them with twine tied to wooden stakes and woven between them. The flowers bloom in late summer and then turn into clusters of 1/4-inch-long pods with seeds inside. When the pods are yellow-brown, clip off the whole clusters and pinch the pods to separate the seeds.

DILL is another cool-season herb that you can plant directly in your garden around the same time that you start peas and salad greens—about six weeks before your last frost date in spring. Like coriander/cilantro, dill has leaves (in this case, ferny, thin foliage) that you can harvest as you need it. You can use the leaves in your aquavit infusion, but for a more potent flavor, wait for the seeds. They are borne on the pale yellow, umbrella-shaped flower clusters that open in midsummer. Dill is an enthusiastic self-sower, too—plant it once, leave the seeds in one or two flowers, and dill will come up in your garden year after year without your help.

FENNEL produces three different harvests, but you can only get two of them from each plant. Belowground, fennel grows a thick, heavy bulb you can roast and eat as a vegetable. Aboveground, the stalk bears ferny leaves with a scent and flavor redolent of licorice. In mid to late summer, a cluster of yellow flowers blooms on top of the stalk, and by the time fall sets in, the flowers have turned to seeds. You can pluck off some of the leaves at any time and use them to flavor meats and side dishes. If you want to eat the bulb, you need to dig it up before the plant flowers, which means that you won't get any seeds. To harvest the seeds, you must leave the bulb in the ground beyond its edible stage. Florence fennel is the best choice for growing bulbs, but bronze fennel is the ideal pick for producing the seeds you want for infusing. If you don't harvest the bulb, fennel is a perennial plant that comes back every season. Plant the seeds directly in the garden in spring after all danger of frost. Once the fennel plants come up, you can ignore them, as they are a very hardy, tolerating both heat and cold. When the flowers have been pollinated, the seeds begin forming. They start out green and slowly turn to brown. Wait for them to finish turning brown before you harvest them, so you get the maximum fennel flavor.

Lightly toasting the seeds of these spices helps to draw out the oils that contain their flavor and aroma before you use them in your infusion. You can toast them in a pan over low heat on a stove or you can put them in an oven with the temperature set at 250°F. In this case, lightly toasting means simply heating them up. Take them away from the heat as soon as you start to smell them. You don't want them to burn even a little or you will taste the charred flavor in your infusion. Use the seeds right away. About 2 teaspoons of each type of seeds is enough to flavor a quart of liquor. For your first couple of batches, use no more than three kinds of seeds, to see how the flavors blend. Start with caraway seeds, as they are the classic flavoring. Use either anise or fennel, but not both, as they have a similar flavor. Let your seedy flavorings steep in the alcohol for three to four weeks.

XXXXXXXXXXX SIMPLE SANGRIAS XXXXXXXXXXX

Fresh homegrown ingredients can perk up ordinary wine and turn it into sangria, a kind of punch that originated as a drink for informal occasions and daily meals in Spain and its former colonies. In its classic incarnation, the base ingredient of sangria was any wine left over in casks at the time of the year when new wine was ready to begin its aging. The added ingredients helped to mask the flavor of different wines blended together. Today you'll find many commercial versions of sangria that are full of artificial flavors and colors and taste a lot like fruit juice with alcohol. You don't have to settle for that because you can easily make it better yourself.

Start with any fruity wine—one you've made yourself is best, but even one you buy with a screw-off lid and no vintage will do just fine. If you want to get more authentic, go with a rioja. Add to the wine any fresh, ripe fruit you have, such as blackberries, blueberries and raspberries, cherries, peaches, plums and apricots, apples and pears, and citrus fruits. Slice the fruit and remove all stems and pits. Make the pieces bite-size, so that you and anyone you share the sangria with can eat the wine-soaked fruit, if you want. Classic sangria is fortified with brandy. You can use liqueurs that complement the fruit, such as Calvados with apples and pears, or peach schnapps with apricots and peaches. Many homemade sangrias have a little added sweetener, such as honey, agave, or a simple sugar syrup. Herbs are not included in basic sangria recipes, but those that mix well with sweet flavors, such as mint, lemongrass, or ginger, add another dimension to the sangria's flavor. Crush leafy herbs with your hands to release their flavors and aromas before adding them to the sangria, but don't cut them into small pieces so they can be culled out before serving. In the case of ginger, cut a few small chunks from the root to float in the liquid. Blend all of your ingredients the night before you want to drink the sangria and let the flavors marry in the refrigerator.

The combinations for making sangria are unlimited and you can often rely on whatever you have on hand. To get you started, here are two ideas that friends have shared with me.

Blend a bottle of rosé wine with a cup of Chambord (black raspberry) liqueur, a cup each of peaches, strawberries, and blueberries, and a handful of crushed lemon or pineapple mint.

For a sangria blanca, blend a bottle of Sauvignon Blanc with a cup of St. Germain (elderflower liqueur), a cup of gooseberries or sliced green grapes, and the juice from one lemon and/or a handful of lemongrass.

LUSCIOUS LIMONCELLO

Limoncello is a traditional liqueur served on the Italian island of Capri, where lemons grow abundantly. It's a light and refreshing drink that's simple for you to make as an infusion with just a few basic ingredients. A friend and cookbook author shared this recipe with me.

He recommends the Amalfi variety of lemon, if you can get them, because they're almost as sweet as they are tart. If you can't get Amalfis, which aren't widely available throughout North America, choose lemons that have a thick rind (I'll explain why that's beneficial) and smell fresh and lemony even before you peel them.

✕✕✕✕✕✕✕✕✕✕✕✕✕✕✕✕ LIMONCELLO ✕✕✕✕✕✕✕✕✕✕✕✕✕✕✕✕

INGREDIENTS
10 lemons

1 liter bottle (about 34 ounces)
190-proof grain alcohol (e.g., Everclear)

3 cups granulated sugar

1. Wash the lemons well in hot water, rinsing several times, to thoroughly remove any wax coating the supermarket added to make them look shiny on the shelf.

2. With a zester, pare off strips of the lemon rind, taking care not to get any of the bitter white pith below skin. You will taste the bitterness if any of the pith gets in the limoncello, so err on the side of caution as you peel. The thicker the rind, the easier this is.

3. Pour the grain alcohol into a glass jar with a tight-fitting lid and add the lemon zest. Put on the lid and set the jar in a cool, dark spot. For the first few days, gently shake or invert the jar once a day to be sure all the lemon rind is distributed evenly.

4. After three weeks, make a syrup by boiling 3 cups of water and thoroughly dissolving the sugar in it. (You can substitute honey for a third of the sugar.) Let the syrup cool and then add it to the lemon infusion. Shake the jar gently to blend the ingredients together. Put the jar back in its cool, dark spot for another week.

5. Pour the fluid through a paper coffee filter or other very fine strainer into another clean jar. Repeat this two or three times, to remove as much of the zest and other particulate as possible. When it's clear, pour it into a bottle. Freeze until it is well chilled, dilute to taste, and enjoy with friends.

CHAPTER № 8

GARDEN TO GLASS

THIS BOOK ISN'T A GARDENING GUIDE. ITS AIM IS TO HELP YOU PRODUCE top-quality fresh ingredients and turn them into your own homemade hooch. As every great vintner and chef knows, how you grow those ingredients is as important to the end result as the care you take after the harvest. You will find pertinent growing information throughout the preceding chapters. These next few pages share the best gardening practices for any crop you're trying to raise.

THINK ORGANIC. You don't have to be a Birkenstocks-and-socks hippie or a celebrity environmentalist to appreciate that whatever you put on your plants may affect its taste. The synthetic fertilizers and pesticides marketed to gardeners are harsh chemicals that leave behind toxic residues (believe that, no matter what claims are made on the packaging). To create the purest, tastiest drinks, pass on the chemicals and take the organic approach.

The organic approach is much more than just rejecting chemicals. The focus is on encouraging the natural processes plants have adapted to. When you collaborate with rather than combat nature, plants are naturally healthy, reach their full productive potential, and have the highest concentration of their all-important flavor compounds. You will be successful if you view your plants as one part of a whole ecosystem that includes the soil, sun, wind, rain, insects, wildlife, and people.

SITE RIGHT. In real estate, only three things matter: location, location, location. The same might be said for gardening. Put a plant where its basic needs are provided for and you'll have very little to do after that. Nearly every tree, shrub, and other plant you grow for harvest needs lots of sun. Fruiting plants need ten hours or more of direct sunlight as they grow and ripen. To fully mature, herbs and grains must have at least six hours of sun during the height of the season. Where you don't have continuous hours of sunlight, you can grow just about any ingredient—even a fruit tree—in a container and move it into the sunshine to get it the light it needs. If a shady spot is all you've got, look for a community garden in your area (www.communitygarden.org is a good place to start) and keep your eyes open for opportunities to forage for ingredients that are valuable to no one else.

Airflow can make all the difference between success and frustration with many plants, but none more so than fruit trees and shrubs. Molds and mildews are fungi that spoil fruit and damage leaves. They thrive in damp conditions, such as in your bathroom, and on plants where moisture sits for hours. Airflow around plants dries them off and reduces the opportunities for fungi to get established. Look for spots to plant where circulation is unimpeded by buildings, fences, and other obstacles, and leave enough room between plants to let air pass between them.

You've seen throughout this book and in many gardening guides the recommendation to plant in well-drained soil. For the same reason that you want air to flow through your plants, you don't want them growing where the ground is always soggy. How well soil drains depends a lot on its content (more on that in the next section), but it also is connected to location. Low-lying areas are prone to collecting rainwater, whereas it drains away from areas at the top of slopes.

A high spot is an ideal location for your garden or orchard for several reasons: It drains well, tends to get more sun, and is breezier than the bottom of slopes. If the site is oriented toward the west or the south—where plants can get the maximum sunlight during long summer days—you have hit the location trifecta.

Many factors, unseen as well as seen, can affect a plant's health. When a plant does not fare well in the conditions you have, especially in more than one season, you can try to alter the conditions or coddle the plant, but that's surprisingly hard to do. Your least frustrating course of action is to choose other plants to grow in that spot.

SOIL SENSE. Consider this: Each teaspoon of healthy soil contains more living organisms than there are people on Earth. The billions of microbes—mostly fungi and bacteria—are invisible to the naked eye, but they have an interdependent relationship with plants. If you make your garden hospitable to them, your plants will be well tended by them. The simple yet very effective way to do that is to feed the microbes and keep them active with a steady supply of dead or dying plants to digest. As they do so, they release nutrients into the soil in exactly the form that plants have evolved to take them up. You can provide the dead or dying plants—organic matter—in the form of dried grass clippings, shredded leaves, straw (but not hay), pine needles, and, best of all, homemade compost.

You can tell when your garden's soil has a healthy microbe population and you don't need a laboratory to do it. Just look for earthworms. They're at the top of the soil food chain and a very reliable indicator that the smaller organisms are alive and well.

Before you add anything other than organic matter to your garden's soil, it's worth taking the time to get it tested. Every state in the United States has a land-grant university that analyzes gardener's soil samples for a nominal fee. Your county has a cooperative extension office—they all do—where you can get information on where and how to get soil tested, along with lots of other valuable information such as your first and last frost dates and best performing varieties for your climate. The results of the soil test tell you how much organic matter is in the soil. If it's 5 percent or more, congratulations—you've been doing a good job of feeding the soil microbes. You'll also find out the levels of two key nutrients—phosphorus and potassium—and the soil's pH. You may have heard advice about adding lime or other "amendments" to your garden soil, but until you've had the soil tested you won't know for sure what it needs.

Most garden plants fare best where the pH is slightly acidic—between 6.0 and 6.5—but blueberries, citrus fruits, and a few other crops adapt best where the soil pH is even more acidic, as low as 5.0. Adding elemental sulfur is a safe way to reduce the pH, if necessary. Only if the test shows your soil has a very low pH—below 5.5—should you add lime, which increases alkalinity.

The ideal soil for growing most garden plants is called loam—it's a mixture of roughly equal parts loose sand and sticky clay, with at least 5 percent organic matter. Not many places naturally have rich, loamy soil. Where the soil is predominantly sandy, it drains quickly, often too fast for plants' roots to absorb the moisture, and it tends to be low in nutrients because they wash out of the soil. Add compost to sandy soil to increase its water retention and bulk up its nutrient levels. Soils high in clay content are dense, so they hold water too well. Loosen up clay soil by adding compost to it.

WISE WATERING. Seeds and new plants must be kept consistently moist, so you may need to sprinkle them daily until they are established and growing. After that, you weaken your plants by watering them a little every day. Instead, switch to deep, infrequent watering. That's about once a week when it hasn't rained. Deep watering encourages the plants roots to go down in the soil to scavenge for water rather than growing near the surface, which dries out more frequently. The best way to water is right on the soil, not on the plants themselves. Leaves don't absorb much water; as I mentioned earlier in this chapter, wet foliage is a breeding ground for mold and mildew. The best time to water is early in the day, so the plants can take it up while the sun is shining. The next best time is about an hour before sunset, allowing time for any excess to dry off before dark. Watering in the middle of the day is wasteful, as much of it will evaporate before the plant has a chance to absorb it.

Trees and shrubs, like other plants, depend on constant moisture to survive from the time you plant them until they are established. It can take a year or two for trees and shrubs to develop their root system, but once they do and have begun a normal growth pattern, these plants do not need to be watered except during extended dry spells.

Their naturally deep roots find the moisture they need far underground. Don't waste water and time irrigating mature trees and shrubs.

Container plants, on the other hand, do need regular watering because their roots cannot draw moisture from deep in the soil. Bear in mind, though, that plants in pots more commonly die from over- rather than underwatering. Water them when they are dry, soak them well, and then let them dry out before watering them again.

FEED WITH CARE. I've already explained that feeding the soil microbes nourishes your plants, and that you feed those microbes with compost and other organic matter. If you do that consistently, you won't need to fertilize frequently, if at all. Plants in containers and seedlings do benefit from the occasional boost from fertilizers made with natural ingredients. Synthetic fertilizers, by the way, tend to be high in salts, which dehydrate soil microbes and over time raise the pH of your soil. (Don't believe any marketing that promises miracles when you use brilliant blue or green liquid fertilizer—what's miraculous is how well nature works on its own.) The best liquid fertilizer is made from fish emulsion (a kind of dead-fish tea) and seaweed. Rich in key nutrients in a form plants can take up as needed, the fertilizer is widely available in home and garden centers. Be sure to use fertilizers, even organic types, sparingly, and follow the instructions on the package. Excessive use of fertilizers contributes to the pollution of fresh water and often causes plants to produce more leafy growth at the expense of fruit.

COMPOST CRAZED. I realize I've mentioned compost quite a bit in this and other chapters, but I'm hoping you'll indulge me for just a few paragraphs more. Compost is the most valuable asset for anyone trying to grow fresh ingredients, whether or not you are committed to the organic approach. It is nature's fertilizer and the most effective soil conditioner. Compost helps maintain constant moisture levels in the soil, by soaking up water like a sponge and dispensing it as needed. Compost also protects your plants from soil-borne diseases, because its active army of beneficial microbes overwhelms the destructive ones.

Making compost yourself could not be easier and it will make you feel good to manage a little of the waste from your home without shipping it off to a landfill. You make compost by blending

Compost

wet, green materials, such as grass clippings, spent garden plants, and kitchen scraps from fruits and vegetables with dry, brown materials, such as fall leaves and straw. You can add crushed eggshells, tea bags, and coffee grounds to compost, but no meat scraps or other animal by-products. Manure from herbivores, such as chickens, rabbits, and horses, adds valuable nutrients to your compost pile, but do not use waste from dogs, cats, or other carnivores (it may carry health-threatening parasites).

When you have piled enough of these ingredients to make a 3-by-3-by-3-foot heap, they begin to decompose rapidly. Every other week or so, use a shovel or garden fork to move the material in the center of the pile that has already decomposed to the edge and shift the unfinished ingredients to the center of the pile. Within a few months, none of the original items will be identifiable. Finished compost looks like dark chocolate cake crumbs and has an earthy, sweet smell.

You don't need a special bin for compost if you have a space on the ground to put the pile—a bin does help to keep your compost pile looking neat for the neighbors. If you don't have a 3-by-3-foot space on the ground, you can buy or make a tumbler-style bin that sits on a frame and has a barrel or other container with a lid into which you put the raw ingredients and spin them around (instead of turning the pile with a shovel). You can even find tumblers in sizes to fit on a patio or balcony.

While you're waiting for your own compost to be ready, you can buy compost in bags at nurseries and home centers. Before you pay, ask to see the product to be sure it doesn't smell like ammonia or contain more sawdust than other organic matter. (These are common problems with bagged compost.)

Compost improves your soil whenever you add it, but it is most valuable as you are planting. After digging a hole or trench, blend it with the soil you've removed and use the blend to backfill once the plant is in the ground. Spread an inch or two of compost around your plants every couple of months during the growing season and just lightly scratch it into the surface to begin its absorption into the soil. That's enough to keep those helpful microbes—and your crops—well nourished and active.

WEED MANAGEMENT. Weeds are kind of like pirates—they show up uninvited and help their scruffy selves to any available food and drink, stealing resources from other plants. If you retaliate with heavy artillery, in the form of herbicides, you risk killing your plants and the microbes they depend on. The most effective defense against weeds is mulch—a thick layer of organic matter that keeps sunlight from reaching weed seeds so they won't sprout up. Dried grass clippings, fall leaves, and straw (not hay, because it contains seeds that sprout into future weed problems) are the best mulches for garden beds. These materials feed soil microbes as they break down. Replenish them throughout the season as they decompose. Bark chips last longer before they break down and are more attractive—they're best for using around trees and shrubs.

Pull weeds that find their way through the mulch while they are young. Every weed that you let flower and produce seeds will leave you with hundreds more of its kind the following season. Be sure to get all of the roots of weeds as you pull them—many can resprout from just a small piece of root left behind. You can put young weed leaves and stems in your compost pile, but discard far from your garden any that have flowered.

PEST CONTROL. You will have insects in your garden; I guarantee it. But before you panic and run off looking for the pesticides, you should know that more than 80 percent of insects do not harm your crops. Many of them survive by eating other insects. And the best way to keep pests from spoiling your hard work is to encourage the food chain—birds, toads, and other insects—to deal with the troublemakers for you.

A simple birdbath in your garden invites your feathered allies to hang around and eat bugs. Toads and other reptiles (yes, including small garter snakes) need a little shelter and an uncultivated area—such as a few haphazardly placed rocks—to move in and feed on pests. Beneficial insects, notably ladybugs and lacewings, hang around gardens, snatching up pest insects for their larvae to feed on. Those beneficials are attracted by herbs and other plants with small flowers. Plant a variety of them around your garden and watch as the good guys flock to it and keep the pests in check.

Planting the same crops in row after row is helpful for farmers, who use mechanical harvesting equipment, but in a garden it makes it too easy for pests to find their favorite food. Instead, mix up your plantings so that if one plant becomes infested, the pests don't find the whole crop. Change the crops you plant in each garden bed from season to season; rotating crops reduces the chance that soil-borne pests and diseases will move in and stay.

The plants most likely to be targeted by pests are those under stress. A healthy plant often can withstand a pest invasion and continue producing its crop. If you do see a plant that's infested, the best strategy is to pull it out and discard it far from your garden.

If you want to take more direct action to save a plant, organic remedies can help you without harming people, pets, or any other living thing but pests. Sticky traps are effective for protecting fruit trees and shrubs. A simple spray you make from a tablespoon of mild liquid dish soap (such as the Ivory brand) and a few drops of cooking oil in a quart of water takes out many soft-bodied insects, such as aphids and mites. For beetles and caterpillars, you can buy a product called Bt (short for *Bacillus thuringiensis*), a naturally occurring bacteria that disrupts the pests' feeding. It's sold in most nurseries and home centers.

REMEMBER TO ENJOY. Growing a garden full of fresh ingredients is a lot like making your own hooch. You will experience surprising successes and frustrating disappointments, unexpected insights and mistakes you will laugh about later. When you put so much care and effort into what you do, the failures can be discouraging. But I promise you that with each growing season and each batch you brew you will gain knowledge and your miscues will become fewer and fewer. Always keep in mind that you do all of this for pleasure. No matter what happens, take the time to savor what you have accomplished—in your garden and in the glass.

RESOURCES

Fermentation Basics

Local winemaking and brewing shops are great places to learn more about the process and get recommendations on supplies from experts and other amateurs. You also will find everything you need from online sources, such as the following.

DeFalco's
Houston, Texas
www.defalcos.com

E. C. Kraus
Independence, Missouri
www.eckraus.com

Home Brewers' Outpost
Flagstaff, Arizona
www.homebrewers.com

Northern Brewer
Minneapolis, Minnesota
www.northernbrewer.com

Winemakers Depot
Jacksonville, Oregon
www.winemakersdepot.com

Four suppliers offer you yeast strains for all kinds of home fermenting.

Lallemand
Montreal, Quebec
www.lalvinyeast.com

Red Star Yeast
Milwaukee, Wisconsin
www.redstaryeast.com

White Labs
San Diego, California
www.whitelabs.com

Wyeast Labs
Odell, Oregon
www.wyeastlabs.com

Cornell University
www.grapesandwine.cals.cornell.edu
Viticulture and enology degree and extension programs.

University of California at Davis
www.wineserver.ucdavis.edu
Viticulture and enology degree and extension programs.

www.extension.ucdavis.edu/unit
/brewing
Master brewer's courses.

Iowa State University
Midwest Grape and Wine Industry Institute www.extension.iastate.edu/wine

YEAST ALCOHOL TOLERANCE COMPARISONS
Journal of Bacteriology, William D. Gray, botany department, Ohio State University, available from the National Institutes of Health Library at www.ncbi.nlm.nih.gov/pmc/articles/PMC518407.

HISTORY OF YEAST RESEARCH
Theoretical Biology of Systems, University of Marseilles
www.bip.cnrs-mrs.fr/bip10/schlenk.htm
This chapter from a book entitled New Beer in an Old Bottle: Eduard Buchner and the Growth of Biochemical Knowledge offers insightful context on fermentation and the research that has grown up around it.

Homegrown Wines

GRAPES
Miller Nurseries
Canandaigua, New York
www.millernurseries.com
Many varieties tolerant of diverse conditions, including a "Wine Lovers Special" combo.

Red Dog Vineyards and Nursery
Ankeny, Iowa
www.reddogvineyards.com
Large selection of cold-hardy hybrids.

BERRIES
Indiana Berry Co.
Plymouth, Indiana
www.indianaberry.com
Berries of all kinds and many varieties to choose from.

Raintree Nurseries
Morton, Washington
www.raintreenursery.com
Vast selection of common and unique berry varieties.

ORCHARD FRUITS
Burnt Ridge Nursery
Onalaska, Washington
www.burntridgenursery.com
Unique fruit tree varieties, including many heirlooms.
Stark Bro's

Louisiana, Missouri
www.starkbros.com
A wide selection of fruit trees from
a vendor with a long history and
sterling reputation.

Southmeadow Gardens
Baroda, Michigan
www.southmeadowfruitgardens.com
Many varieties ideal for winemaking.
A great source for berries, apples, pears,
and more.

CITRUS FRUITS

Four Winds Growers
Winters, California
www.fourwindsgrowers.com
Dwarf and standard-size citrus trees of
all kinds.

Rio Grande Nursery
Mission, Texas
www.rgvnursery.com
Many varieties of grapefruits, lemons,
limes. and oranges

VEGETABLES

W. Atlee Burpee & Co.
Warminster, Pennsylvania
www.burpee.com
The best-known seed company in the
United States offers a wide variety,
including many organic choices.
Ferry-Morse Seed Co.

Fulton, Kentucky
www.ferry-morse.com
You can see its display racks with many
variety choices in retail such outlets as
hardware stores and home centers, or
shop online.

Baker Creek Seeds
Mansfield, Missouri
www.rareseeds.com
A vast selection of heirlooms and other
exceptional varieties, all guaranteed
GMO-free.

Johnny's Selected Seeds
Winslow, Maine
www.johnnyseeds.com
Varieties especially chosen for short
gardening seasons.

Territorial Seed Company
Cottage Grove, Oregon
www.territorialseed.com
Many kinds of organic vegetable seeds
along with berries, fruit trees and more.

INFORMATION

Winemaking Talk
www.winemakingtalk.com
An online community of home
winemakers' sharing their experiences
and helping beginners.

Home Brews

GRAINS

Howe Seeds
McLaughlin, South Dakota
www.howeseeds.com
A variety of grains including barley, in quantities for growing in small spaces.

Peaceful Valley Farm Supply
Grass Valley, California
www.groworganic.com
Organic barley and other grain seeds in quantities for small plots.

High Hops
Windsor, Colorado
www.highhops.net
More than thirty-five varieties of hops rhizomes available in spring, along with other supplies, for home brewers.

Thyme Garden Herb Company
Alseas, Washington
www.thymegarden.com
A choice of organically grown hops

ORGANIZATIONS

American Homebrewers Association
www.homebrewersassociation.org
Find home brew clubs, learn about competitions, search the "Homebrewopedia," ask questions of experts and other users of the online forums, and subscribe to *Zymurgy,* a bimonthly magazine on all things related to homebrewing.

UNIVERSITY PROGRAMS

Washington State University
Extension Service
www.extension.wsu.edu/
maritimefruit/Pages/Cider.aspx
Information on raising cider apples and producing cider on both a commercial scale and in homemade batches.

University of Minnesota Apple Breeding
www.apples.umn.edu
A review of cold-hardy apple varieties for cider and other purposes.

Cornell University
www.ithaca.edu/staff/jhenderson/
apple.html
Apple collection and descriptions.

Cider with a Kick

CIDER AND WINE PRESSES

The Fruit Press
Naches, Washington
www.thefruitpress.com
About $700 for a home-ready setup.

Yakima Press Co.
Yakima, Washington
www.yakimapress.com
Vintage designs.

Greenmantle Nursery
Garberville, California
www.greenmantlenursery.com

Vintage Virginia Apples
North Garden, Virginia
www.vintagevirginiaapples.com

A Honey of a Drink

MEADERIES

B. Nektar Meadery
Ferndale, Michigan
www.bnektar.com
Products can be ordered online and
shipped to customers in the United
States.

Blacksnake Meadery
Dugspur, Virginia
www.blacksnakemead.com

Jilberts Winery
Valley City, Ohio
www.ohiohoneywine.homestead.com

Rabbit's Foot Meadery
Sunnyvale, California
www.rabbitsfootmeadery.com

Redstone Meadery
Boulder, Colorado
www.redstonemeadery.com

Products can be ordered online and
shipped to customers in the United
States.

Sky River Meadery
Sultan, Washington
www.skyriverbrewing.com
Products can be ordered online and
shipped to customers in the United States.

BEEKEEPING AND HONEY
Bee Culture
www.beeculture.com/content/whoswho
A state-by-state (and province-by-
province) listing of local beekeepers,
published by *Bee Culture: The Magazine
of Beekeeping.*

USDA Technical Bulletin 1261
www.libraries.psu.edu/dam/psul/up/
digital/findingaids/724.htm
Published in 1962, by Jonathan White, an
apiculture expert at Penn State University, this is the definitive analysis of the
sugar content, acidity and other attributes of honey from a variety of sources.

GotMead
www.gotmead.com
A comprehensive guide to all things
mead, including user-to-user information exchange and deep access to leading experts for paying subscribers. A
sponsor of the Mazer Cup International.

Mazer Cup International
www.Mazercup.com
The most respected annual mead making competition, open to pros and amateurs.

The National Honey Board
www.honey.com
All kinds of information about the product, including details on using it for homebrewing.

Dare to Distill

SUPPLIES

Home Distilling Equipment
www.homedistillingequipment.com
A variety of different sizes of stainless-steel stills.

Mile High Distilling
www.milehidistilling.com
Equipment and supplies for fermenting and distilling, including parts to assemble your own still and aging barrels.

INFORMATION

Home Distillation
www.homedistiller.org
Information from an experienced enthusiast and an active message board with discussion about all topics related to distilling.

Garden to Glass

SUPPLIES

Gardens Alive
Lawrenceburg, Indiana
www.gardensalive.com
Traps, nontoxic sprays and other organic pest controls, and plant-specific natural fertilizers.

Planet Natural
Bozeman, Montana
www.planetnatural.com
Organic fertilizers, pest control products and composting supplies.

INFORMATION

Organic Gardening magazine
Emmaus, Pennsylvania
www.organicgardening.com
The original and still-authoritative source on growing without chemicals.

The Garden Web
www.gardenweb.com
The Internet's most active and comprehensive gardening discussion group, including user's ratings of gardening product suppliers.

BIBLIOGRAPHY

Homegrown Wines

The Encyclopedia of Home Winemaking by André Vanasse and Pierre Drapeau, Dundurn Publishing, 2005.

From Vines to Wines: The Complete Guide to Growing Your Own Grapes and Making Your Own Wine by Jeff Cox, Storey Publishing, 1999.

101 Recipes for Making Wild Wines at Home by John N. Peragine, Atlantic Publishing, 2009.

Home Brews

The Everything Homebrewing Book by Drew Beechum, Adams Media, 2009.

Making Beer by William Mares, Alfred Knopf, 1994 (revised edition).

The New Complete Joy of Homebrewing by Charlie Papazian, HarperCollins, 1991.

Cider

Cider: Making, Using and Enjoying Hard & Sweet Cider by Annie Proulx and Lew Nichols, Storey Publishing, 1997.

Cider, Hard and Sweet: History, Traditions, and Making Your Own by Ben Watson, The Countryman Press, 1999.

Real Cidermaking on a Small Scale by Michael Pooley and John Lomax, Trans-Atlantic Publications, Inc., 1999.

A Honey of a Drink

The Compleat Meadmaker by Ken Schramm, Brewers Publications, 2003.

Dare to Distill

Home Distillers Handbook by Matt Teacher, Cider Mill Press, 2011.

Moonshine by Matthew B. Rowley, Lark Books, 2007.

Interesting Infusions

Dr. Cocktail: 50 Spirited Infusions to Stimulate the Mind & Body
     by Alex Ott, Running Press, 2012.

Infused: 100+ recipes for Infused Liqueurs and Cocktails by Susan Elia MacNeal,
     Chronicle Books, 2006.

The Seasonal Cocktail Companion by Maggie Savarino, Sasquatch Books, 2011.

Garden to Glass

The City Homesteader by Scott Meyer, Running Press, 2011.

Rodale's All-New Encyclopedia of Organic Gardening, edited by Fern Marshall
     Bradley and Barbara W. Ellis, Rodale Press, 1993.

The Self-Sufficient Life and How to Live It by John Seymour, DK Publishing, 2009.

Uncommon Fruits for Every Garden by Lee Reich, Timber Press, 2008.

INDEX